RICHARD CASTLE | SOLICITOR

DRAFTING GUIDE
FOR PRIVATE LEGAL DOCUMENTS

SECOND **EDITION**

Please send comments on the contents, and suggestions for amendments and additions to schlossmeister@gmail.com.

Mereo Books

2nd Floor, 6-8 Dyer Street, Cirencester, Gloucestershire, GL7 2PF
An imprint of Memoirs Book Ltd. www.mereobooks.com

DRAFTING GUIDE FOR PRIVATE LEGAL DOCUMENTS

978-1467915335

First published November 2011

The address for Memoirs Books Ltd. can be
found at www.mereobooks.com

Typeset in 11/15pt Century Schoolbook
by Wiltshire Associates Ltd. Printed and bound in Great Britain

EXTRACT FROM ACKNOWLEDGEMENTS:
FIRST EDITION

I would like to thank my daughter Alexandra Castle for typing and retyping the drafts of this work and making sense of an untidy manuscript......I express my gratitude to and admiration for the officers of the Office of the Parliamentary Counsel in Whitehall, London. Their drafting guide inspired this work and they freely gave me permission to use their guide. In many instances, the very words here are theirs – I could not improve them.

ACKNOWLEDGEMENTS: SECOND EDITION

For this second edition, I would like to thank the publishers for their commitment and patience; and my wife Dr Mary Schollum for her skill in assembling all the materials and integrating the precedents in the narrative. The novelty of this edition is the introduction of whole precedents, so that the ideas I have put forward in the earlier part of the book can be shown in working form. All the full precedents are of property transactions, and the majority are leases. That is because I practise in those areas, and the precedents have been devised by me and (generally speaking) used extensively by me. They are readily adaptable to fit an infinite number of different circumstances.

I also take this opportunity of paying tribute to the late Trevor Aldridge, whose personal support and pioneering work inspired much in this book.

If any reader would like one or more of the precedents in WORD format, he or she should contact the publishers, or me at schlossmeister@gmail.com.

CONTENTS

PART 1 : CLARITY

PART 2 : POINTS ABOUT LANGUAGE

2.1 WORDS AND PHRASES

2.2 SINGULAR AND PLURAL

2.3 NUMBERS AND DATES

2.4 GENDER NEUTRALITY

PART 3 : DRAFTING TECHNIQUES

3.1 CROSS-REFERENCES

3.2 DEFINITIONS

3.3 PARAGRAPHS

3.4 WORDS INTRODUCING SCHEDULES

PART 4 : VARIATIONS OF EXISTING DOCUMENTS

4.1 INTRODUCTION

4.2 TEXTUAL AMENDMENTS

4.3 NON-TEXTUAL MODIFICATIONS

PART 5 : PERIODS OF TIME

PART 6 : RUNNING ORDER

PART 7 : PRECEDENTS – PRINCIPLES

RT 8 : PLANS

PART 9: PRECEDENTS - EXAMPLES

REFERENCES AND FURTHER READING

FOREWORD

Introduction

1.   This guide has been produced by Richard Castle, a
        solicitor and co-author of *Modern Legal Drafting* (CUP) 2nd
        edition 2006. It is heavily based on the guidance written
        by the Drafting Techniques Group of the Office of the
        Parliamentary Counsel in Whitehall.

2.   The guidance is designed for lawyers in England and Wales
        who need to draft private documents like contracts, leases,
        planning agreements, deeds of various kinds and (though to
        a lesser extent) wills. It is not meant to be a comprehensive
        guide to drafting; nor is it a guide to the interpretation of
        documents or to drafting practice in the past.

3.   Everything in this guide is subject to the fundamental
        consideration that drafts must be accurate and effective,
        and it is recognised that drafters will need to take their
        particular requirements into account. It follows that there
        will be departures from what is said here.

4.   Good examples are printed **blue**, whereas poor examples
        are printed **red**.

Overview

5.   **Part 1** deals with the general drafting principle of clarity.
        Drafters need to think about clarity whenever and whatever
        they draft. Those new to drafting might like to read this part
        in one go (and experienced drafters might like to re-read it
        occasionally).

6.   Most of the remaining parts contain guidance on particular
        points which drafters are likely to come across. The
        intention is that these parts will be referred to as and when
        necessary. Part 9 (new to the second edition) contains
        extensive templates for various transactions.

7.   The need to achieve clarity does of course inform everything
        that is said in the remaining parts. But there are other
        drafting principles which are relevant here too, such as
        effectiveness, consistency and conciseness.

8.   **Part 2** deals with some specific language-related points. In
        particular, there is material on gender neutrality (a separate
        drafting principle in its own right).

9.   **Part 3** addresses some commonly-used drafting techniques.

10.   **Part 4** is about drafting variations of existing documents.

11.   **Part 5** covers the expression of periods of time.

12.   **Part 6** is concerned with the order of provisions in a document.

13.   **Part 7** deals with the use of precedents.

14.   **Part 8** relates to the use of plans.

15.   **Part 9** contains precedents which adopt the principles set out earlier in the book.

PART 1

CLARITY

1.1 INTRODUCTION

(a) Aim of Part 1

(i) Part 1 presents some of the main principles and techniques related to clarity.

(ii) A number of professional drafting offices round the world have produced documents describing ways to improve clarity, including offices in common-law jurisdictions, notably Australia and New Zealand. In the UK, the Tax Law Rewrite did the same, and so have the Scottish Parliamentary Counsel. What is said here draws on material produced elsewhere, in particular the Tax Law Rewrite guidelines and the manual of the Australian Office of Parliamentary Counsel. Above all it derives inspiration from the Office of the Parliamentary Counsel in Whitehall.

(iii) Clarity is one principle of good drafting, but there are others, such as

- effectiveness: fundamentally, your draft must do the job it is intended to do

- consistency: in any one document, using the same term where the same thing is meant; and doing the same thing in the same way, both within a document and, at least for standard provisions, in different documents

- conciseness and avoidance of redundancy: saying what you want to say in the most economical way, but without so much compression that the result is difficult to understand.

(iv)   Part 1 only features clarity. The conclusions reached on
         particular points in the remaining parts are informed
         in part by the need to achieve clarity, but also by other
         drafting principles.

(b)   The principle of clarity

(i)   Clarity is about making it as easy as possible for your
         readers to understand what you are saying.

(ii)   A draft may be clear enough to be effective, but it may still
         be possible to make it easier to understand. That may take
         time, and time is often in short supply. So your aim, more
         precisely, is to make a draft as easy to understand as it is
         possible to make it in the time available.

(iii)   Clarity includes the use of plain language, but also includes
         other things like layout, structure, and typography. Some
         things which can contribute to clarity are not within your
         control when drafting (eg the typeface and line length may
         be a matter for the firm's house style). But other things are
         within your control.

(iv)   Many of the principles and techniques relating to clarity
         may seem obvious. That is because many of them are
         already used by most drafters as a matter of course.

(v)   Not all of the techniques mentioned are applicable in every
         case. Sometimes in a particular case two of them cannot
         both be applied. Sometimes a technique should not be
         used. The approach to be adopted in any particular case is
         a matter for the drafter. But the techniques outlined in this
         book should be among the factors the drafter considers in
         deciding on the approach.

(c)   The test of clarity

(i)   Whether an effort to make a draft easy to understand has
         been successful is tested by whether the intended readers
         in fact find the draft easy to understand. The test of success
         is not whether the approach in Part 1 has been applied.
         It is the interests of the reader, not the use of a particular
         technique, that must guide the drafter.

(ii)   We must never forget our readers. Ultimately, of course,
         they are the people who will be using the document. Their
         requirements may be different depending on who they are.
         A document which is about the assets of an individual (say,
         a will) is likely to have a quite different readership from a
         multi-party regional agreement (say, a construction contract
         for a new railway).

(iii)   But, in addition, we should also bear in mind the
         requirements of professional advisers and the courts. The
         document must be capable of being used effectively from
         day to day, but it must also produce the right result if
         tested in court. And a draft's first readers will often be the
         lawyers on the other side. What one set of readers finds

easy may be quite difficult for another set, or may not be understood by them in the way the writer intended. These competing interests need to be balanced and given due weight in what we write. The weight to be given to different competing interests may be different from instrument to instrument.

1.2 STRUCTURE AND ORGANISATION

(a) Telling the story

(i) Sometimes your reader has no idea what your message is until you deliver it. Yet a party to a commercial agreement will often know, at least in general terms, what the agreement says. So it is especially important to take the reader by the hand and lead him or her in a logical way through the story you have to tell.

(ii) Different readers of a document may be interested in different aspects of the story: for example, a tenant may be concerned about what the rent is and when it must be paid, whereas an estate manager might be more interested in the assessment, appointment and collection of service charges.

(b) Organisation and headings

(i) The clarity of a text is greatly affected by the way it is organised. The reader can be helped by the words you choose for clause headings, subclause headings and (where necessary) paragraph headings.

(ii) It helps if your clause headings give as full an indication of the contents of the clause as you can, consistent with keeping the heading reasonably short (many drafters make sure that their headings do not go into a second line). But a clause heading may not need to repeat the work done by a document heading.

(iii) Headings have a relationship with each other, not just with the clause. Imagine your clause headings as set out in the table of contents; and re-read any table of contents regularly to make sure it hangs together.

(iv) A direction to ignore headings flies in the face of reality and should not be included.

(v) There is a case to be made for using a different but relevant expression in a heading from any used in the text. The technique can highlight meaning, but must be used with care. A wrong heading can confuse, or even alter interpretation.

(c) Schedules

(i) Consider also the division of material into clauses and schedules. Relegating text to the end of the document may not help the reader. It may make break up the story you are telling; or make the structure more complicated than it needs to be.

(ii)   Examples of where a schedule may be useful include—

- technical provision that is unlikely to be of interest to many readers;
- lengthy material that is at something of a tangent to the main story;
- large tables and long lists.

  Other materials which customarily go into schedules are—

- rights granted in leases
- rights excepted or reserved from leases
- forms of documents which might be required later, like authorised guarantee agreements.

(iii) Before putting material in a schedule, however, consider your reader. To have to refer back and forth from definition, to operative part and schedule makes life difficult. Wherever you can, put material on one topic in one place. When that proves impossible, help the reader by signposting where other relevant material can be found.

(d)   Order of material

(i)   *General*

It helps the reader if the material in your document is set out in a logical order, so that later propositions build upon earlier ones.

(ii)   *Forward references*

Reference at any point to material which needs to be understood at that point but which does not appear until later is generally not helpful. This may well be an indication that the material would be better re-ordered. But a signpost to later (or indeed earlier) material which is relevant but which does not necessarily need to be understood now may well be helpful. It can be included in brackets (eg "see clause X").

(iii)   *Overview provisions*

A clause at the beginning of a document or (say) the beginning of a schedule, explaining what is to follow may help the reader to navigate round a larger document where the table of contents is too long to give a clear picture.

(e)   Clause structure

(i)   *Numbering*

Some drafters and house styles favour the decimal system, ie

clause	1
subclause	1.1
paragraph	1.1.1
subparagraph	1.1.1.1

This can be muddling, particularly where the numbers at each level are similar. Moreover, it clutters the line and makes cross-referencing and renumbering a real chore. The following scheme is more straightforward:

clause	1
subclause	1.1
paragraph	(a)
subparagraph	(i) or •

Do not go below a subparagraph. If your text seems to call for a subsubparagraph, recast the text.

(ii)   *Naming*

Resolve to call your four levels in the body of the document clause, subclause, paragraph and subparagraph. It will make reference to a particular provision much easier. In schedules, refer to paragraphs and subparagraphs.

(iii)   *Connection between subclauses*

A subclause is read in the light of a previous subclause in the same clause: it is usually unnecessary in a subclause to repeat material which has been established earlier in the clause.

EXAMPLE

Instead of the following:

(1)   A person may apply to the Council for a permit to play music.

An application under subclause (1) must contain the required information.

(2)   On receiving an application made by a person under subclause (1), the Council may issue a permit to the person.

(3)   A permit issued under subclause (3) must be in the prescribed form.

(4)   A permit issued under subclause (3) authorises the holder to play music as indicated in the permit.

you might say:

(1)   A person may apply to the Council for a permit to play music.

(2)   An application must contain the required information.

(3)   The Council may issue a permit to an applicant.

(4)   A permit must be in the prescribed form.

(5)   A permit authorises the holder to play music as indicated in the permit.

It is helpful if the opening subclause of a clause gives the reader some idea of what the clause is about, especially if the clause introduces a new topic. For example, if the clause produces a particular legal effect if conditions are met, it may be more helpful to state the effect before listing the conditions.

(iv)   *Second sentences*

- Normally each sentence in a clause is a separate numbered provision. But **there is no rule against having more than one sentence in a numbered provision**.

- If every sentence has to be numbered as a separate subclause, the reader may on occasion trip up if the logical connection between subclauses is closer in some cases than others. A second (or even a third) sentence enables the drafter to distinguish two levels of connection between subclauses in the same clause; or to deal with cases where putting a second thought in a separate provision would place undue emphasis on it.

    EXAMPLE

    (1) A party to this contract has the right to refer a dispute arising under the contract for adjudication under a procedure complying with this clause.

    For this purpose, "dispute" includes any difference.

    (2) A party may give notice to the other parties of his intention to refer a dispute to adjudication, after which...

- In this example, there are only two main propositions - the right to refer disputes to adjudication and what happens in referrals. The point about the meaning of "dispute" is just an afterthought to the first, and it might be unhelpful to treat it as equal in weight to the other two.

(f)   Clause length

(i)   Many drafters try to avoid clauses containing more than ten subclauses or so (and some are stricter than that).

(ii)   However, this is again a matter of judgment: if you have a self-contained story to tell, it may be more convenient for the reader to have it all in one long clause, rather than in two or more shorter clauses.

(iii)   It may also help if the division into clauses follows the division of thought. If, for example, you have to make separate provision for three different cases, but one case requires more provision than the other two, it might still be easiest to have only one clause for each case, even if that means that one of the clauses is longer than you would otherwise wish.

1.3   CLARITY OF EXPRESSION

(a)   Sentences

(i)   *Keep propositions short*

- A large slab of unbroken text is difficult to understand. Many drafters try to avoid subclauses or undivided clauses of more than, say, half-a-dozen unbroken lines.

- Clarity is helped by the use of short sentences (but not so short that the result is distracting). A long sentence may require the reader to keep too much in the mind, although it can be made easier to understand by paragraphing. But a single complex proposition is sometimes best expressed in a single sentence (with paragraphing, if appropriate) rather than as a series of short sentences in successive subsections, if that avoids making the reader reconstruct the single proposition in order to make sense of it.

- All this is sometimes expressed as an exhortation to write, not necessarily short sentences, but short "sense bites"[1] - that is, information should be presented to the reader in short bites: each of them may be contained in a separate phrase or paragraph which grammatically amount together to a single (longer) sentence.

- A single sentence with subordinate clauses is often harder to understand than a series of sentences expressing the same substance. So a single sentence should ideally contain one idea only, or be split into sense bites each containing one idea only. For example, qualifications or conditions can be split off into separate subsections or even into separate clauses.

(ii)   *Paragraphing*

- Paragraphing is an obvious way of making a sentence more digestible, by separating out bite-size chunks. However, paragraphing can be overdone. It is distracting to the reader if the paragraphs are too short or break up the flow of the sentence.

- Many drafters avoid descending to subparagraphs, so as to avoid requiring the reader to hold too much in the mind. The point at which sub-paragraphing impedes understanding is quickly reached. Drafters of private documents frequently overlook this.

- For more on paragraphs, see part 3, *Paragraphs*.

---

1. For longer exposition, see Butt *Modern Legal Drafting* p.182.

Paragraph headings in a subclause

•   An alternative to paragraphs is to use sub-headings
     within a subclause.

EXAMPLE

5.   RENT REVIEW

5.1   Review dates

The rent is to be reviewed on the ▶[fifth, tenth and fifteenth]
anniversaries of the beginning of the term; and "review
period" means the ▶ [second, the third or the fourth] ▶[five]
years of the term, as appropriate.

5.2   Rachet provision

For any review period, the revised rent is to be
whichever is the greater of—

(a) the new rent ascertained in accordance with
     this clause, and

(b) the rent payable immediately beforehand.

5.3   Proceedure

(a)   The new rent for a review period may be agreed at any
       time between the Landlord and the Tenant.

(b)   In the absence of agreement and not more than six
       months before the end of the relevant ▶[five] years of
       the term, the Landlord may opt to have the new rent fixed
       either by an arbitrator or a valuer.

(c)   An arbitrator must act under the Arbitration Act 1996, and a
       valuer must act as an expert and not as an arbitrator.

(d)   The Landlord may apply to the President of the Royal
       Institution of Chartered Surveyors for the nomination of an
       arbitrator or a valuer.

5.4   Principles for fixing new rent

(a)   Market rent

       The new rent is to be the yearly rent at which the Property
       might reasonably be expected to be let at the relevant review
       date, with the assumptions set out in (b) but disregarding the
       matters set out in (c).

(b)   Assumptions

       The assumptions are that—

       (i) the Property is available to let on the open market without
           a premium with vacant possession by a willing landlord to
           a willing tenant

> (ii) the term of the notional letting is ▶[five] years
>
> (iii) the Property is to be let as a whole and subject to the provisions of this lease other than the amount of rent but including the provisions for rent review.

- Use sentences that are simply and logically constructed (the classical structure is subject-verb-object). If possible, avoid inserting words between the subject and the main verb.

  EXAMPLE

  Instead of—

  > The Landlord may, if the required conditions are met, issue a licence to the Tenant

  you could say—

  > The Landlord may issue a licence to the Tenant if the required conditions are met.

- In a sentence which contains a main proposition that depends on a number of conditions, the reader may be better served by putting the main proposition first, rather than putting the conditions first.

  EXAMPLE

  > A notice must be given if—
  >
  > > (a)...
  > >
  > > (b)...
  > >
  > > (c)...

  is probably easier to understand than—

  > If—
  >
  > > (a)...
  > >
  > > (b)...
  > >
  > > (c)...
  >
  > a notice must be given.

  The latter also offends against the "avoid sandwiches" principle (see part 3, *Paragraphs*, para. (c)).

- Parallel phrases in the same sentence can be hard to understand: that is, phrases which start and finish with the same words but which have no particular relationship with each other. These require the reader to keep what are in effect two or more different possible sentences in mind simultaneously, and can often be impossible to grasp without unpacking the whole idea.

- This can happen, for example, with two phrases ending with prepositions but then attaching to the same subsequent text.

9

EXAMPLE

the provision of services by means of, or in association with the provision (by the same person or another) of, an electronic communications network

This needs to be unravelled, for example as follows.

the provision of services—

(a)   by means of an electronic communications network, or

(b)   in association with the provision (by the same person or another) of an electronic communications network

(b)   Positive and negative

(i)   The positive is often easier to understand than the negative version of the same thing.

EXAMPLE

Speak after the tone

is easier to understand than—

Do not speak until you hear the tone

(ii)   But this is not a universal rule: it depends on the nature of the proposition and on the overall effect of what is said. A prohibition may well be best expressed in the negative.

EXAMPLE

Do not walk on the grass

is probably easier to grasp at once than—

Walk only on the pathways

(iii)   Negatives are often better avoided when expressing a quantity.

EXAMPLE

not less than 25%

might be more clearly expressed as—

at least 25%

or

25% or more

(iv)   It is generally agreed that it is best to avoid double negatives. But it may not always be possible to do so.

EXAMPLE

The Landlord has not acknowledged that no application was made

does not mean the same as—

The Landlord has acknowledged that an application was made

(c)   **Active and passive**

(i)   It is usually clearer to use the active voice than the passive voice.

EXAMPLE

The Tenant must give a notice

is more quickly grasped than—

A notice must be given by the Tenant

(ii)   But the passive may be appropriate if the agent is unimportant, universal or unknown.

EXAMPLE

If a notice is given to the Tenant...

might be appropriate if the same rule applies whoever gave the notice.

(iii)   The passive may also be useful as a technique for gender-neutral drafting (see part 2.4 *Gender neutrality,* para. 2.4).

(d)   **Verbs and nouns**

A verb form is often easier to understand than the noun form of the same proposition.

EXAMPLE

A party may apply

is crisper and more instantly intelligible than—

A party may make an application

(e)   **Possessives**

The traditional style would be to say "of the", as in "of the council"; but it is usually easier to understand the shorter form with an apostrophe: "the council's".

(f)   **Vocabulary**

(i)   Use language that does not call attention to itself, whether by being fastidiously old-fashioned or self-consciously modern. The reader should be considering your message, not how you deliver it.

(ii)   That means writing in modern, standard English as far as possible, avoiding archaisms and other words or phrases which can give rise to difficulty. However, it is also not the drafter's role to be in the vanguard of linguistic development: the language we use should reflect ordinary general usage.

(iii) But it may sometimes be necessary or most economical to use a technical legal expression (for example, "hereditament" in connection with rating, or "fee simple" in connection with property). Common words like "facilities" are often difficult to find alternatives for. (See also part 2.1, *Words and phrases*)

(g) Tone and emphasis

(i) Adopt a moderate, level tone. Brevity is good but brusqueness is not. Clarity is not served by giving the reader a jolt.

(ii) In particular, speak firmly but don't shout. Excessive emphasis may be distracting.

EXAMPLE

An applicant must provide all of the following information

is not an obvious improvement on

An applicant must provide the following information

(iii) See also part 2.1, *Words and phrases*.

(h) Adaptation to style of amended instrument

(i) Drafters who are faced with amending an earlier instrument have different views about how hard they should try in their amendments to adopt the linguistic register of the document being amended. The older the document being amended, the more likely it is that this question will arise.

(ii) Some drafters do not make the attempt at all; others do so to a greater or lesser extent. Either way, clarity need not be sacrificed for the sake of an invisible join between the old and the new text; and the approach to adopt may be influenced by the need to avoid ambiguity.

(i) Tables

A table is often a clear way of setting out a sequence of events, a list of relative proportions (eg in a shared ownership lease) or a number of cases with the rule that applies to each of them. Yet as with anything else, tables can be overdone.

(j) Formulas

(i) As an alternative to a narrative approach, formulae are perfectly acceptable when used appropriately. A formula may be the neatest way to express a relationship between various quantities; spelling the same thing out in words may be the very worst way of expressing it.[2]

(ii) However, sometimes a sequence of written instructions may be more accessible than a formula: see, for example, the method statement, discussed below.

---

2   See Butt *Modern Legal Drafting* p.159; and *Chartbrook v Persimmon Homes* [2009] UKHL 38.

(iii)   And if the proposition is very simple (for example, the sum of two quantities) using a formula may make it look more complicated than saying the same thing in words.

(iv)   A formula may be more accessible to, say, a surveyor, an actuary or accountant than to a general reader. So be guided by the expected readership.

(k)   Method statements

(i)   A "method statement" may be the neatest way to set out the various steps in a process.

EXAMPLE

How relief works

This clause explains how the deductions are to be made.

The amount of the relievable loss to be deducted at any step is limited in accordance with clause [ ].

Step 1

Deduct the relievable loss from the profits of the trade of the final tax year.

Step 2

Deduct any part of the relievable loss not deducted at Step 1 from the profits of the trade of the previous tax year.

Step 3

Deduct any part of the relievable loss not deducted at Step 1 or 2 from the profits of the trade of the tax year before the previous one.

Step 4

Deduct any part of the relievable loss not deducted at Step 1, 2 or 3 from the profits of the trade of the tax year before that one.

Other claims

If the relievable loss has not been deducted in full at Steps 1 to 4, the person may use the part not so deducted in giving effect to any other relief under this deed [etc]

(l)   Conditions

(i)   One drafting device which has possibly not received the attention it deserves is the condition technique, widely used in United Kingdom statutes. The condition technique is a tool for shortening sentences and making the passage more easily understood. The drafter first shortly states in a subsection that the general rule is expressly subject to conditions. Those conditions (sometimes called cases) are then set out in following subsections. This technique is illustrated (in this instance by using 'cases') in section 191 of the Income Tax (Earnings and Pensions) Act 2003.

EXAMPLE

191   Claim for relief to take account of event after assessment

(1)   A claim may be made for relief in the following cases.

(2)   The first case is where —

    (a)   the tax payable by an employee for a tax year in respect of a loan has been decided on the basis that, for the purposes of section 175 (benefit of taxable cheap loan treated as earnings), the whole or part of the interest payable on the loan for that year was not paid, and

    (b)   it is subsequently paid.

(3)   The second case is where —

    (a)   the tax payable by an employee for a tax year in respect of a loan has been decided on that basis that, for the purposes of section 188 (loan released or written off: amount treated as earnings), the loan has been released or written off in that year, and

    (b)   the whole or part of the loan is subsequently repaid.

(4) The third case is where —

    (a) the tax payable by an employee for a tax year in respect of a loan has been decided on the basis that -

        (i) section 288 (limited exemption of certain bridging loans connected with employment moves), and

        (ii) section 289 (relief for certain bridging loans not qualifying for exemption under section 288), will not apply because the condition in section 288(1)(b) (which requires that the limit on the exemption under section 287(1) has not been reached) will not be met, and

    (b) that condition is met.

(5) Where a claim is made under this section the tax payable is to be adjusted accordingly.

(ii) The condition technique is an extension of the methods recommended by English barrister George Coode in the middle of the nineteenth century.[3] It ought to be more widely used. Alienation and forfeiture clauses in leases (for instance) could then be made much more digestible.

FIRST EXAMPLE

8.2   Assignment of whole

(a)   General rule

The Tenant may assign the Property as a whole if the Tenant first —

    (i) obtains the written consent of the Landlord in the form of a licence to assign under seal (and that licence is not to be unreasonably withheld)

    (ii) satisfies the circumstances referred to in (b), and

    (iii) complies with the conditions set out in (c).

The circumstances and conditions are prescribed for the purposes of the Landlord and Tenant Act 1927 section 19(1A).

(b)   Circumstances

The circumstances referred to are:

    (i) all sums due from the Tenant under this lease must be paid up to the date of the assignment

    (ii) in the reasonable opinion of the Landlord, there must be no material breaches of any of the tenant covenants in this lease at the date of application for licence to assign

---

3   *On Legislative Expression* 2nd edition 1852 (London: Thomas Turpin) reproduced in Stanley Robinson *Drafting* 1980 (London: Butterworths) p. 331.

   (iii) in the reasonable opinion of the Landlord, the proposed assignee must be a person who is likely to be able to comply with the tenant covenants in this lease and to continue to be able to comply with them after the assignment.

  (c) <u>Conditions</u>

   The conditions referred to are:

   (i) if reasonably required by the Landlord, a rent deposit equivalent to up to six months rent must be paid to the Landlord, and the assignee will enter into a rent deposit agreement substantially in the form set out in schedule 3

   (ii) if reasonably required by the Landlord, before the assignment and before giving occupation to the assignee, the outgoing Tenant must enter into an authorised guarantee agreement substantially in the form set out in schedule 4

   (iii) if reasonably required by the Landlord on assignment to a company, the assignee must ensure that at least two directors of the company or some other guarantor or guarantors reasonably acceptable to the Landlord enter into direct covenants with the Landlord in the form of guarantor's covenants contained in this lease

   (iv) on completion of the licence to assign, the outgoing tenant or the assignee must pay the Landlord's reasonable legal costs and surveyors' fees incurred in preparation of the licence to assign and associated documents.

SECOND EXAMPLE

32. TENANT'S RIGHT TO BREAK

32.1 Provided the precondition below is met, the Tenant may terminate this lease by [▶three] months notice to the Landlord given—

  (a) after the expiry of the first [▶six] months of the term, and

  (b) before the start of the last [▶six] months of the term.

32.2 Subject to the preceding subclause, the notice may expire at any time and not necessarily on a day for payment of rent.

32.3 The precondition is that on or before the expiry date of the notice, the

Tenant must—

(a) have paid to the Landlord all rent and other sums due up to and including the expiry date of the notice

(b) have complied with the electricity inspection and gas servicing clauses of this lease, and

(c) give vacant possession of the Property.

32.4 As soon as practicable after the termination, the Landlord will refund to the Tenant any rent or other payment relating to a period after the termination.

PART 2

POINTS ABOUT LANGUAGE

2.1   **WORDS AND PHRASES**

(a)   **"and"**

(i)   This relates to the use of *and* at the beginning of a sentence.

(ii)   There is no reason in principle to rule out the use of *and* at the start of a proposition. However, it should not so be used unless there is a real need for it - and it is hard to think of examples where there is a real need. Unnecessary use of *and* is at best clutter and it may distract the reader by excessive emphasis (see the section on tone and emphasis in part 1.3).

(iii)   If two propositions are so closely connected to each other as to need an *and*, there may be a case for putting them in the same numbered provision (perhaps in two sentences).

(b)   **"and/or"**

Avoid[4]

(c)   **"and"**

(i)   Beware of a proliferation of *any*'s. In many cases *a* or *an* is just as good. Again, there are too many *any*'s in many private documents.

(ii)   *Any* can be ambiguous.

EXAMPLE

The Council must consult any organisation appearing to be representative of substantial numbers of allotment holders

Is this any one organisation or all organisations?

---

4   See Butt *Modern Legal Drafting* p.286.

(iii)   *Any* may be useful—

- to emphasise that something is of universal application or without qualification (but only where it is really necessary to do so);

- to refer to both a singular noun and an uncountable one (eg any document or information).

(d)   "being"

(i)   The *being* formula to define something is cumbersome and archaic. It can often be avoided by the use of a different construction.

EXAMPLE

Instead of -

A person who is served with a notice, being a person who has a right over the property, may serve a counter-notice

you could say -

A person who is served with a notice and has a right over the property may serve a counter-notice

(ii)   Occasionally the *being* formula, the masculine and the feminine, and the singular and plural are all necessary to give meaning to unknown possibilities. This is particularly the case with wills. Take for example the common provision for grandchildren:

EXAMPLE

I give my estate in equal shares to my children A, B & C. But if any of my children has died before me, leaving a child or children alive at my death, then that child or those children (being my grandchild or grandchildren) is or are to take, equally if there is more than one of them, the share in my estate which his, her or their parent would otherwise have taken

This is a rare example of a simple concept being necessarily expressed in a complex way.

(e)   "best endeavours"

Avoid these words (and their cousins "reasonable endeavours") at virtually any cost. You are only storing up trouble.[5]

(f)   "but"

(i)   There is no rule against putting *but* at the beginning of a sentence, and it can on occasion be helpful.

(ii)   But it should not be overused. Unnecessary or over-emphatic words distract the reader (and see *Tone and emphasis* part 1.3).

(iii)   An initial *but* is unnecessary if it is in any event obvious that the second statement qualifies the first. For example, a proposition to the effect that "Nothing in this clause applies" or "Clause (x) does not apply" does not need an initial *but*.

---

5   See Butt *Modern Legal Drafting* p. 244; and *Jet2.com Ltd v Blackpool Airport Ltd* [2012] EWCA Civ 417.

(g)   **"follows", "as follows", "the following"**

A colon does not have to come after any of these words. In fact, sentence construction is often easier if they precede a full stop, particularly if the list is more than one or two shortly-expressed things.

EXAMPLE

1.   DEFINITIONS

1.1.   The following definitions and expressions apply throughout this lease.

1.2.   "The Property" is The Primrose Building, Beaulieu, Anytown shown edged red on the attached plan.

1.3.   "The term" is five years beginning 1 September 2021.

1.4.   "The insured risks" are fire and such other risks as the Landlord may from time to time consider it desirable to insure against.

1.5.   The expressions "landlord covenants" "tenant covenants" and "authorised guarantee agreement" have the same meanings as in the Landlord and Tenant (Covenants) Act 1995.

(h)   **"here"- words**

(i)   *Hereby* should not be used unless there is a particular reason for concluding that the inclusion of the idea conveyed by *hereby* would or might serve a useful purpose. Even then, if you really need to emphasise that something is being done by virtue of your proposition, consider using words such as "by this deed" instead.

(ii)   Other *here-* words should not be used.

(i)   **"only"**

Avoid placing *only* where it will produce ambiguity.

(j)   **"or"**

(i)   *Or* can have an inclusive sense (A and/or B) as well as an exclusive one (either A or B but not both), especially in a provision which gives permission or confers a power.

EXAMPLE

The landowner may require the employer to—

              (a) produce any relevant document, or

              (b) provide any relevant information

(ii)   In that example, it seems very unlikely that the powers are intended to be mutually exclusive. But in other cases it may be less clear, as perhaps the following example illustrates.

EXAMPLE

The landowner may require the employer to

    (a) pay a fine, or

    (b) take action of a description specified by the regulator

(iii)   So a degree of caution is in order. It may in particular be possible to make the intention clear by the introductory words. See also part 3.3 *Paragraphs.*

(k)   **"shall"**

(i)   Shun *shall.* It is antique and can be ambiguous.

(ii)   There are various alternatives to *shall* which can be used, depending on context:

- *must* in the context of obligations (although "is to be" and "it is the duty of" may also be appropriate alternatives in certain contexts);

- "there is to be" in the context of the establishment of new bodies etc.;

- use of the present tense in provisions about application, effect, extent or commencement;

- "is amended as follows" in provisions introducing a series of amendments;

- "ceases to have effect" in the context of total revocation.

(iii)   A reason for not departing from *shall* might be that it would appear in text to be inserted near to existing provisions that use *shall* in the same sense.

(l)   **"subject to"**

(i)   To say that "This clause is subject to clause x" is not always helpful. It may be better to be more precise about the relationship between the propositions (eg "This clause does not apply to... (see clause x)".

(ii)   It may also be possible to use another expression: for example, "but see clause X". Or it may be possible to state briefly the case to which a different rule applies by saying, for example, "except" or "unless" (as in "Unless the person concerned is under 30".)

(iii)   The relationship between the provisions may be particularly hard to follow if *subject to* is at the beginning of the sentence. It may be better to start with the main proposition and then indicate that there is a qualification (perhaps in a second sentence).

(iv)   Alternatively, it may be possible to dispense with *subject to* altogether, especially if the qualifying proposition is close to the proposition it qualifies - in which case the reader may be expected to grasp the relationship between the two without extra help.

(v) "Subject to what follows" and "subject as follows" are potentially ambiguous and should be avoided unless it is abundantly obvious from the context exactly which of the following provisions are being referred to. Where there is any doubt, specify exactly which provisions you mean (or express the relationship in some other way).

(vi) Global cross-references such as "Subject to the provisions of the telecommunications code" are sometimes unavoidable but may not be entirely meaningful to non-expert readers. If the reference cannot be avoided, try to include an indication of where the relevant other provision is made.

(vii) See also part 3.1 *Cross-references* - and in particular the injunction to draft by reference to substance rather than by reference to the provision in which it is contained (para. 3.1(a)(iii)).

(m)   "such"

Avoid *such* where possible. Often *the* or *a* will do just as well

EXAMPLE

Instead of

on such day as the Owner may specify

you might say

on a day specified by the Owner

(n)   "there"- words

(i) *Therefrom* and *therewith* are archaic and should not be used.

(ii) Other *there-* words should only be used where the advantages of doing so outweigh their old-fashioned ring, there is no obvious more modern alternative and the meaning of the reference back is clear.

(o)   "where" (and "if")

(i) *Where* is useful for stating a case or a set of circumstances in which a later proposition applies. *If* is used for stating a contingency.

(ii) So *where* may be better for cases which inevitably will occur, *if* for conditions which may or may not be satisfied.

(iii) There is of course no clear-cut distinction. In some cases, it may depend on from whose perspective you are looking at the situation.

EXAMPLE

Suppose a landowner has power to serve notices on defaulters—

Where the landowner serves a notice on an occupier, the landowner must...

(here we are speaking of the landowner, who will frequently serve notices)

but

If the landowner serves a notice on an occupier, the occupier must...

(here we are speaking of the occupier, for whom the notice is not at all inevitable).

(p) **"which"**

Correct your computer program where necessary when it suggests that *which* in relation to a relative clause must be preceded by a comma.[6]

(q) **"whilst"**

Use *whilst* sparingly. Whilst it can be deployed to introduce a contrast, it is often no more than a kind of poetic version of *where*.

2.2 SINGULAR AND PLURAL

(a) Local authorities and other bodies corporate should be treated as singular nouns.

EXAMPLE

If the Council is satisfied that the conditions are met, it may...

(b) When textually amending a document that uses the plural, it may be necessary to follow suit in order to avoid confusion.

2.3 NUMBERS AND DATES

(a) **Cardinal numbers**

(i) Figures should normally be used for all numbers above 10.

(ii) Figures should also normally be used for numbers up to and including 10 that relate to sums of money, ages, dates, units of measurement or in quasi-mathematical contexts.

(iii) In other contexts, whether numbers up to and including 10 are spelt out or expressed as figures depends on what seems more natural or appropriate in the contexts concerned.

(iv) A number that begins a sentence should normally be spelt out (but it is probably best to avoid beginning a sentence with a number in any event).

(v) Mixing words and figures referring, in a single context, to things of the same kind should be avoided.

(b) **Ordinal numbers**

(i) Ordinal numbers above 10th should not be spelt out.

---

6   For more details, see Castle *Relative Clauses: the that/which debate*, Clarity no 50, November 2003, p.35.

(ii)   Whether ordinal numbers from 1st to 10th are spelt out should be decided in the light of what seems more natural or appropriate in the contexts concerned. But see below for dates.

(c)   Percentages

"%" should be used rather than "per cent".

(d)   Dates

Numbers should be used.

2.4   GENDER NEUTRALITY

(a)   The principle of gender neutrality

(i)   It is now generally accepted that as far as possible a drafter (and note the use of "drafter" rather than the older "draftsman") should write in a gender-neutral way

(ii)   The private drafter has customarily relied upon the Law of Property Act 1925 section 61, which provides that unless the context requires otherwise, in all private documents the masculine includes the feminine and vice versa.

(b)   Practical application

(i)   In practice, gender-neutral drafting means two things.

•   Avoiding gender-specific pronouns (such as "he") for a person who may be either male or female or, in the case of a legal person who is not an individual, neither.

•   Avoiding nouns that take a form that appears to assume that a man rather than a woman will hold a particular office, do a particular job or perform a particular role: "chairman" is the most obvious example.

(ii)   A flexible approach is called for.

(iii)   There will be some documents where gender-specific drafting will remain appropriate (eg in deeds about marriage or divorce).

(c)   Amending existing documents

(i)   One obvious case where exceptions may need to be made is in amendments of existing documents. Although it may often be possible to use gender-neutral techniques to frame textual amendments of provisions that were originally framed in gender-specific terms, there are clearly going to be cases in which that will not be possible. Sometimes, it would be necessary to rewrite a provision from scratch in order to make a very minor amendment in gender-neutral terms. That could obscure the real purpose of the amendments.

(ii)   Similarly, references in an amending instrument to a "chairman" mentioned in the instrument to be amended would have to refer to that office by the name that it was given in the earlier document.

(iii)   For instance, documents relating to the custody of a child may well be drafted entirely on the assumption that the caring parent is the mother and that the absent parent is the father. When amending that documentation any reversal of the assumption would have to be crystal clear and might have to be done by a substantial rewrite.

(d)   Individuals and offices

(i)   If a document refers to a specific individual, gender neutrality does not require his or her gender to be concealed.

(ii)   A similar practice however should not be followed in relation to office holders (eg "the incumbent of the Parish of St Clements"', because references to "the office holder" without more are not normally references to any particular individual.

(iii)   Different considerations might apply where the current holder of a specified office (eg the Chief Executive) is clearly identifiable.

(e)   Achieving gender neutrality: nouns

(i)   The gender-specific noun most likely to be encountered is "chairman".

(ii)   Possible replacements include "chair" or "person appointed to chair".

(iii)   It may be possible to use a different word entirely, such as "convenor" or "president", but these might perhaps have different connotations.

(iv)   There are some words for offices, functions and jobs which do not end in "man" and which might be regarded as gender-specific because of the existence of alternative female forms. These should be regarded as gender-neutral.

(v)   For example, "testator", "executor", "manager" and "actor" should all be regarded as gender-neutral, despite the existence of "testatrix", "executrix", "manageress" and "actress".

(f)   Achieving gender neutrality: pronouns

(i)   The remainder of this part illustrates possible ways of avoiding gender-specific pronouns ("he", "his" and so on).

(ii)   The techniques discussed are not exhaustive. Nor are they "recommended approaches". They are just examples of techniques that have in fact been used. Readers should form their own judgment about them.

(iii)   *Repeat the noun*

•   You can repeat the noun rather than using a pronoun.

EXAMPLE

Notices affecting the Property

If the Tenant receives a communication from a competent authority or likely to affect the Property, the Tenant must—

(a) immediately send details to the Landlord

(b) without delay, take all reasonable steps to comply with the communication at the Tenant's expense

(c) join with the Landlord in making any representation to the communicating authority reasonably required by the Landlord.

- Constant repetition of a noun or phrase in a way which would not occur in speech is unlikely to be thought to be "plain English" and might detract from readability.

- This is particularly the case with a long phrase like "the Detective Chief Superintendent", where in speech one would instinctively say "he" or "she".

(iv) *Use a defined term*

- It may be possible to use a defined term for a lengthy official title (for example, "the Chancellor" for the "Chancellor of the University of Bradford", or "the Vicar" for the incumbent of a parish.

- This kind of approach reduces, but does not entirely eliminate, the awkwardness of a repeated noun. Consider whether it is really worthwhile to require the reader to substitute the actual wording intended for the defined term: it may only be worthwhile if the actual wording is long and would have to be repeated a lot.

- Care also needs to be taken that the alternative noun does not import an unwanted or tendentious meaning.

(v) *He or she*

- For individuals you can of course say "he or she".

EXAMPLE

...had he or she not died...

A person holds and vacates office as a member of the Council in accordance with the terms and conditions of his or her appointment

...an application by her or him for child support maintenance...

- In many ways this is a natural solution. But it is only possible for individuals, not bodies corporate or unincorporated associations.

- Some may object that "he or she", in that order, still betrays a gender bias (though sometimes the context may suggest a case for the feminine pronoun preceding masculine, as in the child support example above).

- There is also an objection that to refer to both genders means using words technically made unnecessary by the section 61 of the Law of Property Act 1925.

- It can be awkward where "he or she" needs to be repeated a lot. "Himself or herself" is particularly unsuitable for frequent repetition.

(vi)   *He, she or it*

- Where a non-natural person needs to be referred to as well as an individual, this is possible. But it is likely to be cumbersome unless used very sparingly.

(vii)   *They etc*

- Some documents use "they" or "them" as a third person singular pronoun.

    EXAMPLES

    ...references to the time at which a person is notified are to the time at which they are first given notice...

    The chair of the Commission holds office as chair...in accordance with the terms of their appointment

- This use of the plural pronoun is thought by some to be grammatically incorrect, though it reflects common usage and is well-precedented in respectable literature over several centuries.

- This usage may be less obtrusive in the case of *them* or *their*. *They* may require a verb in the plural form, which some readers may find disconcerting.

- Given the mismatch between singular and plural, care needs to be taken that "they" or "them" clearly relates to the noun in question.

(viii)   *Plural noun followed by "they"*

- Draft in the plural.

    EXAMPLE

    The rules may provide that participants may only carry on activities if they hold a permit

- Section 61(c) of the Law of Property Act 1925 (singular includes the plural, and vice versa) may facilitate use of this technique. But take care to ensure that the plural does not allow in an ambiguity that would be avoided if the singular were used.

(ix)   *Replace the noun with a letter*

- Rather than finding an alternative noun, it may be possible to use a letter.

  EXAMPLE

  If a person ("S") who is registered under this deed as a service provider in respect of activity carries on that activity while S's registration is suspended, S is disqualified from acting

- Use of a letter in place of a noun is not exactly "plain English". It requires the reader to go through the mental hoop of substituting the actual noun being referred to and may thereby decrease readability. Consider whether this is worthwhile if the letter is used only a few times; or replaces a noun which is itself reasonably short. There may of course be other reasons for using letters - in formulae, or where the drafter is referring to two or more people of the same description (person 1 and person 2).

- If a letter is used, it should be reasonably intuitive, eg "P" for purchaser, "V" for vendor, rather than random tags eg "A" and "B". But again take care not to use a letter which might have unwanted connotations (eg "V" for victim, even if the word "victim" is never used).

(x)   *Substitute "the" or "that" for the personal pronoun*

- Avoid the personal pronoun by using an article.

  EXAMPLES

  "local police area" means the police area in which the home address is situated

  the reasonableness or otherwise of that belief (not his belief)

  The Chief Executive may remove a member if satisfied that the member has without reasonable excuse failed to discharge the duties of membership

- This approach on occasion may risk losing the link between the noun and the person being spoken of and thereby lose clarity, or at least may give the reader an unexpected jolt.

(xi)   *Omit the pronoun*

- It is not always necessary to use a pronoun at all.

EXAMPLES

circumstances which justify doing so (not circumstances which justify his doing so)

immediately before death (rather than immediately before his death)

- This technique relies on the reader using the context to supply the omitted pronoun. Care is needed to ensure that resulting proposition does not become uncertain, apply too widely or read unnaturally; and to ensure that the omission does not affect the operation of caselaw to supply the meaning of the phrase concerned or the meaning as generally understood by readers (and lawyers in particular).

(xii)   *Omit the phrase which requires the pronoun*

- It may be worth considering whether the phrase requiring the personal pronoun is really worth having.

EXAMPLE

The Leader of the Council may...

rather than

The Leader of the Council may, if he thinks fit...

- This involves taking a view as to the redundancy of the words omitted. Obviously care needs to be taken to ensure that the omission does not affect operation of caselaw or sit unhappily with approaches adopted elsewhere in deeds being varied.

(xiii) *Use the passive*

- Use of the passive to avoid gender-specific writing has its attractions, but excessive use of the passive is usually thought to detract from readability (see part 1.3, *Active and passive*).

EXAMPLE

explaining why the rules have been broken

rather than

explaining why he broke the rules

(xiv)   *"Who" instead of "if...he"*

EXAMPLES

This clause applies to a jobholder who...

A person commits an offence who...

A person who—

      (a) obstructs a person acting under authority

      (b) remains on the reserve, or

      (c) enters the reserve

      commits an offence

One danger of the approach in the last example is that it postpones the operative words to the end, making the conditions a "sandwich" in the middle of the sentence. That can distract from readability if the conditions go on for too long.

(iv)   *Impersonal constructions*

EXAMPLES

It is an offence for a person to...

A member may be removed from office on any of the following grounds—

      (a) failure to discharge the functions of membership;

      (b) failure to comply with the terms of appointment;

      (c) conviction of a criminal offence

Again, care needs to be taken not to produce an unnatural dislocation between the person and the thing or event being spoken of.

(v)   *Use a present or past participle*

EXAMPLES

Before giving such guidance... (rather than Before he gives....)

A person is not to be taken to have a conflict of interest for these reasons alone:

      (a) being or having previously been engaged...

PART 3

DRAFTING TECHNIQUES

3.1 CROSS-REFERENCES

(a) Use of cross-references

(i) Cross-references can prove particularly hard work for the reader, so it is helpful to minimise their use. This can sometimes be done by re-ordering the material.

(ii) When a new clause or subclause is inserted in a draft, cross-references may need renumbering. This provides another reason to cut out cross-references whenever possible. Where cross-references are appropriate, consider replacing clause numbers with a description.

EXAMPLE

If the parties are unable to agree within two months (and time is of the essence of this) the clause in this deed headed 'DISPUTE RESOLUTION' applies.

(iii) Generally, it is helpful to refer to a substantive rule or proposition, rather than the provision containing it (in which readers are unlikely to be interested).

EXAMPLE

Suppose clause (1) says—

(1) A company must pass a resolution before [doing something].

You want to make an exception for small companies.

You could say—

(2) Subclause (1) does not apply in the case of a small company.

But rather than telling readers about "subclause (1)", it might be more helpful to say—

(2) No resolution is required in the case of a small company.

(iv)   If a cross-reference by number is absolutely necessary, it is made more user-friendly by adding words describing the effect of the provision referred to.

EXAMPLE

...subject to the Tenant complying with condition 11.12 which relates to discharges into drains.

As a bonus, the description may well save your bacon if you have made a mistake with the number.

(b)   Parenthetical descriptions

(i)   It will generally be helpful to provide a parenthetical description of a provision referred to. But the drafter will need to consider the usefulness of the descriptive words against the disadvantage of interrupting the flow of text.

(ii)   The parenthetical description is a description, not a quotation. It will often be the heading of the clause referred to, but it does not have to be. For example, the heading may have been devised in the context of other headings in the document, but may not be particularly helpful taken in isolation.

(iii)   It should be made clear whether the parenthetical description relates to a particular subclause or other portion of text, or whether it relates to the clause generally. In the latter case, it may be helpful to use a formulation along the following lines:

EXAMPLE

In clause 1 (description of the property), in subclause (1)...

instead of

In clause 1(1) (description of the property)....

(c)   "above" and "below"

(i)   Do not use "above" and "below" unless it is appropriate to do so for the purpose of achieving internal consistency or certainty. "Above" or "below" it may help to produce certainty, or at least clarity, if you are referring in one breath to a provision of the document and a provision of another document.

(ii)   The convention that variations should follow the style of the document amended does not need to be followed in connection with the use of "above" and "below", particularly in the case of substantial insertions of new text.

(d) **"of this deed", "of this clause", "of this schedule" etc**

(i)   As a general rule, these expressions should be avoided.

(ii)   They may serve a useful purpose in contexts where "above" or "below" might otherwise be used (see above): there may be reasons of symmetry or emphasis which mean that, for example, "of this agreement" is to be preferred to "above" or "below".

(e) **"schedule to this deed"**

The recommendations relating to the use of "above" and "below" apply equally to references to a schedule "to this deed".

(f) **Arabic and Roman numerals**

For variations of a document in which Roman numerals have been used, it is clearer to continue to use Roman numerals.

3.2   DEFINITIONS

(a) **Kinds of definition**

(i)   Definitions are broadly of four kinds, as follows.

    (1)   Definitions of major concepts without which the reader cannot understand what follows. For example, what is meant by "the property" and "the term" in a lease.

    (2)   Definitions adopted for the sake of drafting convenience.

        EXAMPLE

        In this deed, "the 1954 Act" means the Landlord and Tenant Act 1954

        Definitions of this kind should be kept to a minimum. They are likely to be less convenient to the reader than to the drafter.

    (3)   Definitions of words or expressions which will be understood in general terms, but where a degree of certainty or clarification is needed.

        EXAMPLES

        In this agreement, "child" means a person under the age of 18

        In this deed, "statute" includes subordinate legislation

    (4)   Definitions making, for convenience, a minor adjustment of what a word or phrase would otherwise mean.

        EXAMPLE

        In this agreement, "employment" includes self-employment

        This kind of definition should also be used sparingly.

(b) Where to put definitions

(i) Definitions should be devolved to the bundle of clauses, the clause or the subclause in which they are used. Only these terms used throughout a document need to be put in a general definitions clause. Even then, it may not be necessary. Above all, avoid putting all definitions of any type in the same clause. It is a real hindrance to the reader.

EXAMPLE

1. BACKGROUND

1.1 By an agreement ("the option agreement") dated 25 May 2016 made between the Grantor and the Grantee, the Grantor granted to the Grantee an option to buy land to the rear of 2 Dotton Fields, Anytown on the terms set out.

1.2 By an assignment dated 23 February 2017 made between the Grantee and the Option Holder, the benefit of the option agreement was assigned to the Option Holder.

1.3 Since the date of the option agreement, the Grantor has acquired additional land in the vicinity, and the parties have agreed to vary the option agreement as follows.

2. PROPERTY

2.1 The Property in the option agreement is the land to the rear of 2 Dotton Fields, Anytown shown edged red on the plan attached to this agreement ("the new plan").

2.2 The new plan is to be regarded as "the Plan" for the purposes of the option agreement.

(ii) Where the defined term is used more than once—

• a definition of the first and second kind referred to above should normally be defined up front, as the reader will not understand what is being said. So it should appear either in the first place where the defined term appears or, if more convenient, in an introductory definitions provision.

• a definition of the third kind referred to above can usually be left to the end;

• a definition of the fourth kind referred to above can also usually be left to the end, unless there is a danger of the reader being seriously misled.

(iii) Definitions which are given up front should be indexed so that the reader can see in one place whether the term is defined or not. This does not apply if the defined term is used only once.

(iv) A good interpretation section therefore includes—

- index entries for definitions that have already been given (eg "In this agreement, x has the meaning given in clause 3", and

- minor definitions of the third and fourth kinds referred to above.

(v)   Avoid prospective definition: "In this clause and the next clause, x means y". The reader of the next clause may not see the definition. If necessary, repeat the definition.

(c)   One-off definitions

Where the defined term is used only once, the definition should appear in the same provision (eg the same clause). Contrary to what is sometimes said elsewhere, one-off definitions can often be extremely helpful. Take this simple rule, for example:

(1)   Adventure jet boats that operate on braided rivers must be fitted with a structure which allows emergency exit for all persons when the boat is inverted on solid level ground.

(2)   A **braided river** is a river flowing in a number of channels separated by stable or unstable bars or shoals.

Conventional wisdom would have the one-off use of "braided river" combined with the main rule, producing something like:

Adventure jet boats that operate on rivers flowing in a number of channels separated by stable or unstable bars or shoals must be fitted with a structure which allows emergency exit for all persons when the boat is inverted on solid level ground.

That is just about acceptable, unless "braided river" has a particular resonance for a large proportion of the intended audience. The technique would not be acceptable if the necessary definition of the chosen term was much longer.

(d)   Choice of label

(i)   Avoid labels which are misleading (and, conversely, do not give defined terms a meaning the reader would not expect).

EXAMPLE (to avoid)

In this deed, references to assignment include subletting

(ii)   A defined term should ideally in itself give the reader some clue about what it means.

EXAMPLE

An AGA would be a better label for an authorised guarantee agreement than a guarantee.

(iii)   Equally, colourless terms such as "the relevant person" should where possible be replaced with something more helpful.

(iv) Similarly, for letters denoting persons or concepts, it may be best to choose a letter relating to the thing denoted: so, for "the tenant" perhaps "T" rather than "X".

(v) Using the same label to denote different things in the same document will inevitably confuse.

(e) Operative provision in definitions

It is bad practice to include operative material in a definition. Definitions that overlook this principle are sometimes referred to as "stuffed definitions". As an example, in a definition of "the term" it would be wrong to specify the circumstances in which a party could bring the term to an end prematurely.

(f) Definitions involving cross-references

(i) If a document is to use a term which has already been defined in the way desired in another document, it may be useful to borrow the definition from that other document.

(ii) There are at least two ways of doing this, for example:

In this deed, "health care" has the same meaning as in the principal agreement (see clause 98)

In this deed, "health care" has the meaning given by clause 98 of the principal agreement

(iii) The first approach may be the only possible one where the meaning of the word or phrase in the earlier document is not given in a single place but has to be constructed from a number of different provisions. This approach may also be better if the definition has been elaborated on by case law which you want to attract.

(iv) In other cases, the second formulation may be better as more concise. But consider then whether it would not be even better just to copy the definition out.

(g) Lists of definitions

(i) Sometimes it makes sense to list definitions in conceptual order (eg where each definition builds on the previous one). Think of a document dealing with the business of jet boats. It proves necessary to state (or define) what is meant by "boat" "jet boat" "adventure jet boat" and "non-adventure jet boat". If these are dealt with alphabetically, the reader does not know what is meant by a "boat" when he or she reads the interpretation of "adventure jet boat". The problem is compounded if all definitions in the documents are lumped together in one alphabetical list. The solution is to separate related definitions into a subgroup and then move from the general to the particular or the more particular. So in our example, the heading might be "Meaning of 'boat' and related expressions" and the order in which the items are dealt with would be (1) boat (2) jet boat (3) adventure jet boat (4) non-adventure jet boat, Similar examples are legion, for instance "substance", "noxious substance" and non-noxious substance".

(ii) In most cases, though, definitions should be listed alphabetically. Definitions involving numbers (eg "the 2002 Act" means the Enterprise Act 2002) should appear first.

(h)   **Other technical points**

(i) "Unless the context otherwise requires" is not helpful. Do not use it at all if there is no case where the context does otherwise require - and in such a case, it may be better to say what is meant in that context.

(ii) Some writers deplore the use of a definition which is used only in another definition, unless that is the only way to make the other definition manageable.

(iii) It should be clear to which portion of the resulting document the definition will apply: so use "in this contract", "in this clause" and so on unless there is no possible doubt.

(iv) For the most part it is not obvious that "*for the purposes of this deed*, x means y" has any particular advantage over "*In this deed*, x means y".

(i)   **Capitals in definitions**

Although the habit is ingrained in most private drafters, there is absolutely no need to capitalize every defined term. In fact, it is distracting and destroys the flow of the sentence for the reader. See the following, for instance.

Not to Commence Development in respect of any Housing Parcel without having obtained the written approval of the Council to an Affordable Housing Specific Scheme for that Housing Parcel such scheme to be submitted for approval simultaneously with the submission of the first Reserved Matters Application for that Housing Parcel

Keep capitals for the beginning of sentences and for proper nouns (ie names of people or bodies).

(j)   **Indexes**

Consider using an index of defined expressions. This is far better than the customary long dictionary-type list of definitions all in one place.

(k)   **Description rather than definition**

It is often clearer to describe a process rather than define it. Most private drafters only define nouns or noun phrases. Sometimes you need to say what an adjective or an adjectival phrase means.

EXAMPLE

4.   TERMINATION EVENTS

4.1   If any of the events specified in the following subclause occurs, this agreement ceases to have effect. Thereupon the whole of the arrears due at that time under the lease become payable immediately.

4.2   The following are specified events for the purposes of the preceding subclause:

(a)   The Tenant assigns the lease with profit. The lease is assigned "with profit" if is assigned in association with payment of a premium to the Tenant or with disposal by the Tenant of goodwill, trade fixtures, chattels or stock.

(b)   The Tenant sublets the whole or substantially the whole of the property demised by the lease with profit. A subletting is "with profit" if it is made in association with—

(i)   a rent greater than the rent then passing under the lease

(ii) payment of a premium to the Tenant, or

(iii) disposal by the Tenant of goodwill, trade fixtures, chattels or stock.

3.3   PARAGRAPHS

(a)   Introduction

(i)   An obvious way of making a sentence more digestible is to separate the text out into numbered paragraphs (as described in part 1.3 *Clarity of expression*).

(ii)   Drafters should though be careful not to overdo paragraphing. Just because text can be turned into paragraphs doesn't mean it has to be. In some cases it may be better to have continuous text, and not to separate out the items at all.

(b)   Two sets of circumstances

(i)   Do not put two or more sets of circumstances with differing outcomes in the same sentence (eg in the same subclause).

EXAMPLE (to avoid)

If the Main Contractor considers that—

(a)   a subcontractor is not likely to achieve the target, or

(b)   a subcontractor is not likely to achieve the target in a reasonable time, the Main Contractor may after consulting the subcontractor—

(a)   revise the target, or

(b)   require the subcontractor to explain

(ii)   Instead, split the proposition into two so that there is one series in each paragraph.

EXAMPLE

(1)   If the Main Contractor considers that a subcontractor is not likely to achieve the target, the Main Contractor may after consulting the subcontractor revise the target.

(2)   If the Main Contractor considers that a subcontractor is not likely to achieve the target within a reasonable time the Main Contractor may require the subcontractor to explain.

(c)   "Sandwiches"

(i)   The following structure is a sandwich—

If an inspector reasonably believes that

(a)   premises falling within this deed are unfit for human occupation,

(b)   they are nevertheless occupied, and

(c)   the life or health of the occupants is at risk,

the inspector may serve a notice under this clause.

(ii)   This structure can impede understanding. It is often possible to move the proposition in the full-out words at the end so that it appears in the opening words. The result is then easier to follow. Instead of the text above, you could say this—

An inspector may serve a notice under this clause if the inspector reasonably believes that—

(a)   premises falling within this deed are unfit for human occupation,

(b)   they are nevertheless occupied, and

(c)   the life or health of the occupants is at risk.

(d)   Conjunctions

(i)   Ensure that it is clear whether the paragraphs are intended to operate cumulatively or as alternatives (and see part 2.1, *Words and phrases*).

(ii)   There should not be a mixture of conjunctions, ie different conjunctions at the ends of different paragraphs in the same provision.

(iii)   *Cumulative or alternative paragraphs*

- Where a provision is paragraphed, the intention may be that the paragraphs are to operate cumulatively, or it may be that they are to operate as alternatives. In either case, it is up to the drafter to ensure that the intention is readily apparent to the reader.

- So far as "or" is concerned, the drafter is confronted with the linguistic problem that "or" can have both a cumulative or an inclusive sense (ie a reference to A or B means either A or B or both) and an alternative or exclusive one (ie a reference to A or B means either A or B but not both). Dickerson[7] suggests that: 'Observation of legal usage suggests that in most cases "or" is used in the inclusive rather than the exclusive sense'. This construction may be bolstered, or alternatively excluded, by the context.

EXAMPLE

Keep open for trade

The Tenant must remain open for trade during the usual shopping hours for the class of business carried on by the Tenant. The Tenant is not required to keep open for trade in any period during which—

    (a)   the Tenant is carrying out authorised fitting-out works or other alterations

    (b)   it is not possible to occupy the Property following damage or destruction by an insured risk; or

    (c)   occupation or trading would result in breach of another provision of this lease.

Here, the first "or" is alternative, whilst the second is cumulative.

- It may be tempting to omit "or" from provisions in order to avoid any suggestion of exclusivity and perhaps to make it clear from the opening words what is intended. But where it is obvious from the context that the provisions would be read in an inclusive sense, it may be better from the point of view of clarity or consistency to follow normal English and use "or".

- Sometimes it will be desirable to spell out that both of two alternatives are a permissible option. For example, a provision allowing a landlord to require reinstatement of the property or claim damages might be construed as disallowing both. So if both may be wanted, it would be best to say so.

---

7. Dickerson *Fundamentals of Legal Drafting* p.106.

- Similar issues can arise with "and". If a court were given power to order that treatment be given to an animal *and* that it be sold or destroyed, would it have to do both? Again, though, the context will probably supply the answer.

(iv) *Use of single conjunction*

- Often it will be sufficient to put the appropriate conjunction at the end of the penultimate paragraph and rely on the implication (in the absence of a contrary indication) that each of the preceding paragraphs is separated by the same conjunction.

- However, if the "and" or "or" appears only at the end of the penultimate paragraph, the reader has to wait until then to know whether the paragraphs are cumulative or alternative. This is may be unhelpful with a long list of paragraphs.

- Avoid "and/or". It has been judicially condemned[8] and can easily lead to misunderstanding.

(v) *No conjunction*

- It is also possible to avoid a single conjunction by making it clear in the opening words whether the paragraphs are cumulative or alternative.

  EXAMPLE

  A person who applies for a permit must send a copy of [all] [at least one] of the following documents:

  (a) birth certificate;

  (b) passport;

  (c) driving licence.

- This can be heavy-handed in simple propositions, when "and" or "or" may be better.

(e)   Punctuation

(i)   In the case of a simple list of paragraphs linked by a conjunction, commas or semi-colons may be used.

(ii)   If the paragraphs are followed by full-out text that is effectively a continuation of the proposition contained in the text preceding the paragraphs, commas should be used, not semi-colons (see the example of a "sandwich" above).

(iii)   Semi-colons may be more appropriate than commas where there is no conjunction ie where the paragraphs are in effect a list setting out matters that have no particular affinity with each other.

(iv)   Sometimes lists can end with no punctuation at all.

---

8. See eg *Bonitto v Fuerst Bros & Co Ltd* [1944] AC 75 at 82.

(f)   Unnumbered paragraphs (lists)

Lists need not have numbers or letters. A list of things may be sometimes usefully displayed as paragraphs without numbers or letters, especially if the list is not too long and the entries are relatively short

3.4   WORDS INTRODUCING SCHEDULES

Introductory words for schedules are always helpful, and should be used. Examples for a lease are:

Rights granted

Rights excepted and reserved (rather than simply Exceptions and reservations)

Form of rent deposit agreement

Form of authorised guarantee agreement

Tenant's works

PART 4

VARIATIONS OF EXISTING DOCUMENTS

4.1 INTRODUCTION

Deeds of variation should be much more direct than they customarily are. In most of them, there is too much unnecessary verbiage and leaping about, to and from definitions, operative part and schedules.

4.2 TEXTUAL AMENDMENTS

(a) Operative words

(i) Insertions and substitutions

- The following forms are acceptable—

  imperative form: after x insert y / for x substitute y

  declaratory form: after x there is inserted y / for x there is substituted y

- In each case the effect of the variation is clear.

- Where a single clause makes provision for a series of amendments (as opposed to a single amendment) to a document or to a clause, the first clause is often in a declaratory form, while the remaining propositions are in the imperative:

  (1) The [principal deed] is amended as follows...

  (2) In clause 1, after subclause (1) insert....

- Although the effect is clear, there is something to be said for using the same form in both the opening proposition and the amendments.

(ii)   *Revocations*

- The following formulations, or variations of them, are often used to make textual amendments to a document by the revocation of one or more provisions or words within the document—

  omit x / x is omitted

  x ceases to have effect

  x is revoked

- Here the imperative form is possible only with "omit".

- For revocations of less than a whole document, all of these are acceptable, regardless of the unit of text being repealed. Clearly only "is revoked" or "ceases to have effect" would be used for a whole document. It might then make for consistency to use "is revoked" or "ceases to have effect" (rather than "omit") for smaller units of text.

- To use "is revoked" would also be consistent with "revoked" schedules.

(b)   How much text to substitute

(i)   In most cases it will be helpful to the reader of the amending document, or the reader of the document being amended, to substitute more text than is strictly necessary. For example—

- where a number of related changes are being made to a single provision,

- where the end result of a group of amendments would be to alter the whole basis of an existing provision or to leave very little of the previous text,

- where it is otherwise helpful to the reader to substitute a few extra words.

(i)   In some cases a parenthetical description may help instead.

(c)   Parenthetical description

(i)   Generally, see the discussion of parenthetical descriptions in part 3 *Cross-references*, para (b). In this section, only aspects relevant to textual amendments are discussed.

(ii)   It is helpful to give a brief description of the provision that is being amended, to give the context of the amendment and perhaps its significance. The parenthetical description will often be the heading of the clause or schedule, but it does not have to be - it may be better, for readers of the amending document, to describe the clause in a different way.

(iii)   To describe the clause or schedule which is being amended may help to explain the significance and context of the amendment, but is unlikely of itself to tell the reader exactly what the amendment does. To tell the whole story you probably need to describe the particular portion of text which is being amended, whether a subclause or a smaller subdivision. But it will not be practical, or necessary, to do that in every case.

(iv)   For an important substantive amendment, it may be worth taking the reader by the hand and explaining the entire context, so that the meaning of the textual amendment is then readily apparent. But it is difficult to sustain this on a consistent basis in an amending document of any length. There is certainly no point in giving a description of a subclause unless it actually helps the reader to understand the amendment.

(d)   Amendment of headings

(i)   It is often useful to amend the heading to a provision.

(ii)   In particular, it may be helpful to do so if the provision is falsified by a textual amendment.

(iii)   There is no need to amend a heading merely because the existing heading is not quite what you would have chosen for the amended text.

(iv)   There are also examples of cases where a heading needs to be changed without there being a change to the text under the heading. One example is where a parallel set of provisions is added after existing provisions and there need to be headings that distinguish and connect the neighbouring sets of provisions.

4.3   NON-TEXTUAL MODIFICATIONS

(a)   Non-textual modifications and textual amendments

By "non-textual modification" is meant a modification to a document that is not intended to result in a change to the text of the modified document (in contrast to a textual amendment, which is).

(b)   Need to avoid formulations used in textual amendments

The best approach to avoid the reference to substitution altogether

EXAMPLE

Clause 3 is to apply to subcontractors as well as employees but as if—

(a) in subclause (1) the reference to wages was to earnings; and

(b) in subclause (2) the reference to 3 months was to 6 months

(c) **"Modification"**

Incidentally, the use of the word "modification" does not of itself exclude the possibility that what is intended is a textual amendment.

EXAMPLE

There follows an extract from a well-drafted deed of variation to an option agreement relating to land.

5.5   In paragraph 3 (75 Dotton Fields) under the heading "Patio" for the words "To the immediate rear of the flats" substitute:

> "To the immediate rear of the flats or such other area as the tenant may request,".

5.6   Insert the following paragraphs after paragraph 5:

"6   47 & 49 Dotton Fields

Fence

Install from point K to point L, and then on to point C and then on to point J on the Plan a 1.8m high close-boarded fence consisting of 2.4m x 100mm x 100mm concrete posts concreted in at 2.7m centres with 3 no. cant rails, 150mm deep wood gravel boards and 1.65m feather-edged boards

7.   51 & 53 Dotton Fields

Fence

Install from point M to point N on the plan (which is to be taken as being to the rear of the store on the 51/53 boundary) a 1.8m high close-boarded fence consisting of 2.4m x 100mm x 100mm concrete posts concreted in at 2.7m centres with 3 no. cant rails, 150mm deep wood gravel boards and 1.65m featheredged boards (the fair face of the fencing to face 51 Dotton Fields). All the timber is to be pressure-treated brown, the fence posts being on the Council's property at 53 Dotton Fields."

6.   TRANSFER VARIATION

6.1   The draft transfer in the fifth schedule to the option agreement is to be varied as follows.

6.2   The Plan is to be the new plan.

6.3   In clause 13.2.2.1 (fence line responsibility of the transferee) for the words "points marked J, C, B, D and H on the Plan" substitute:

> "points marked H, D, B, K, L, C and J on the Plan, the fence posts being on the Property".

7.   CONFIRMATION OF OTHER PROVISIONS

In all other respects, the provisions of the option agreement and the draft transfer are confirmed.

PART 5

PERIODS OF TIME

5.1 INTRODUCTION

This part considers some aspects of expressing periods of time. It assumes that in deciding how to describe a particular period the drafter's objectives are:

- to ensure that it is certain when the period begins and ends;

- to ensure that the reader has the greatest chance possible of telling from the words used when the period begins and ends, rather than having to refer to case law;

- to express the period as simply as possible.

5.2 START OF PERIOD: FRACTIONS OF DAYS

(a) A document often needs to describe a period by reference to some event. An example is a period of 14 days during which an appeal may be made, where the "event" is the decision to which the appeal would relate.

(b) In this example, it might be supposed that the appeal period should run from the decision. But this would cause problems, because the decision will have been made part-way through a day, and if the appeal period is to be expressed in whole days (or weeks, months or years) it has to begin at the beginning of a day. The question is, which day? Instructions are not always clear on this point.

(c) It may well be wrong in policy terms for the period to start running from the beginning of the day *after* the day of the decision, because that would disallow an appeal made on the day of the decision.

(d)   If the period starts with the beginning of the day of the decision, it will technically include the part of that day that precedes the decision (during which an appeal will of course be impossible). This may not in practice cause any problems. But if the appeal period is short (for example, 7 days) it may be worth considering whether as a matter of policy the number of days should be increased by one, to take account of the fact that the period starts to run on the day of the decision and not the next day.

(e)   Appeal periods are of course not the only periods that give rise to this kind of question. It may not always produce the right result to begin a period at the beginning of the day on which a particular event occurs: each case needs to be considered on its own merits. And it will be obvious when some periods should start (for example, a year beginning with 1 April), so fractions of a day are not always an issue.

5.3   "BEGINNING WITH", "FROM", "AFTER"

(a)   A clear way of expressing a period of, for example, 14 days so that it starts at the beginning of a particular day is to describe the period as "14 days beginning with" the day in question.

(b)   Alternative methods are to refer to a period of 14 days "from" or "after" a particular event.

(c)   The proper construction of "14 days from [the event]" will depend on the context. As a general rule, this wording will be taken to *exclude* the day on which the event takes place. This is something of which the user of the document may very well be unaware.

(d)   "14 days after [the event]" will also generally be taken to exclude the day of the event (*Dodds v Walker* [1981] 2 All ER 609) but this will also depend on the context.

(e)   It is suggested that "14 days *beginning with*" the day of an event (or any other day or date) is often the least ambiguous short way of ensuring that the period starts to run at the beginning of that day.

(f)   References to a period "ending with" a particular day or date are equally unambiguous.

(g)   A reference to a period "beginning *on*" or "ending *on*" a particular date or day would not give the same certainty, because it would leave open the question of the time at which (on the day in question) the period begins or ends.

(h)   A reference to "14 days from" a point that is bound to occur at midnight (for instance, the end of a year) makes clear exactly when the 14 days are to begin and end: in such a case "from" is as unambiguous as "beginning with".

5.4 **"THE PERIOD OF"**

Deeds and documents have often referred to (for example) a 14 day period as "the period of 14 days". In many cases the words "the period of" do not add anything and could be omitted - the reference could simply be to "14 days". If a reference back is needed, it may be possible to refer to "those 14 days" instead of to "that period".

5.5 **"WITHIN", "BEFORE THE END OF"**

(a) Contracts often require something to be done "within" a particular period or "before the end of" a particular period.

(b) A requirement to take an action "before the end of 3 weeks beginning with [a particular date]" would apparently allow the action to be taken at any time up to the end of those 3 weeks, including at any time before the 3 weeks began. A requirement to take the action "within" those 3 weeks would limit the time in which the action may be taken to those 3 weeks.

(c) In some cases, the effect of either wording will in practice be the same. An example would be where a copy of a document is required to be given within/before the end of 3 weeks beginning with the date when the document comes into existence. But in other cases, the different wordings may produce materially different results.

(d) A requirement to do something "by the end of" a period would seem to amount to the same thing as a requirement to do it "before the end of" the period.

5.6 **UNITS OF TIME**

(a) Periods of time are commonly expressed in days, weeks, months or years. Which unit of time to use will depend sometimes on the policy and sometimes on the drafter's decision. Obviously, the longer the period, the less helpful it will be to use short units of time. For example, it is suggested that all readers will know that 30 days is about a month, but that a period expressed as (for example) 150 days would be much less readily understandable.

(b) Months are a particular problem because of their varying length. Section 61 of the Law of Property Act 1925 defines a "month" as a calendar month, but this appears to do no more than prevent it from being interpreted as a lunar month. When a period of "one month" begins other than at the beginning of a month, when does it end?

(c) According to the rule in *Dodds v Walker* [1981] 2 All ER 609, where an application had to be made "not more than 4 months after" the giving of a notice on 30 September 1978, the last date for making the application was 30 January 1979. The date of 30 January 1979 is arrived at by treating the 4-month period as—

(i)   beginning at midnight between 30 September and 1 October 1978 (that is, excluding the rest of the day on which the notice was given, according to the rule mentioned in paragraph 5.3(d) above), and

(ii)   expiring at the end of the day in January 1979 corresponding to the day in September 1978 at whose end the period began - that is, day 30. (If the period had been expressed to be "4 months beginning with" the date when the notice was given, the last date for making the application would have been 29 January.)

5.7   THE CORRESPONDING DATE RULE

(a)   The rule in *Dodds v Walker* is known as "the corresponding date rule". Under it, the length of a period of "1 month" varies according to when the period begins. For example, a period of "1 month" beginning at midnight on 4/5 April, which will end at midnight on 4/5 May, will be shorter than a period of "1 month" beginning at midnight on 4/5 May (because April is shorter than May).

(b)   The corresponding date rule obviously cannot apply unmodified in all cases, because the months of the year do not all have the same number of days. *Dodds v Walker* confirmed that where (for example) a period of 1 month starts at the end of 30 January, it ends at the end of 28 February, or in a leap year 29 February. The difficulty and its solutions can be expressed in tabular form, as follows.

Triggering event on	Expiry in 30-day month on	Expiry in February on
29th	29th	Last day of the month
30th	Last day of the month	Last day of the month
31st	Last day of the month	Last day of the month

(c)   Because the corresponding date rule can be a trap for the user, in some cases it may be worth considering whether a period of (for example) 3 months would be better expressed as 12 weeks or 90 days. The periods expressed in these ways will not be identical, but whether this matters will depend on the context.

5.8   NON-WORKING DAYS

(a)   Some contracts exclude certain days (for example, Saturdays, Sundays and bank holidays) from specified periods. Others make no distinction between holidays and working days. If a specified period is very short, it may be worth remembering that weekends and bank holidays will not be treated differently from other days unless express provision to this effect is included.

(b)   If any non-working days are to be excluded from a period, consideration needs to be given to exactly which days these should be. It should be remembered that bank holidays are not the same in different parts of the United Kingdom, also that some days which are popularly thought of as bank holidays are not in fact so (for example, Good Friday, and Christmas day except in Scotland).

(c) Schedule 1 to the Banking and Financial Dealings Act 1971 lists some bank holidays, but not all. Bank holidays may be created by royal proclamation - the early May bank holiday is an example.

PART 6

RUNNING ORDER

6.1 GENERAL

(a) Group clauses by topic rather than (for example) by the person on whom an obligation is cast.

(b) As far as possible, keep material on similar topics together, though usually in a separate clause.

6.2 BOILERPLATE

(a) The term 'boilerplate' is used for those provisions of a document which are necessary but do not form part of the core provisions. Boilerplate will therefore often remain unread, and may never come into play at all. Boilerplate will differ from one document to another. So will the order of clauses. Where a standard precedent is used, it is often safer to tack a clause on the end rather than risk a mistake with cross-references. The boilerplate clauses in a lease might run as follows—

Inspections and viewings

Suspension of rent if property destroyed or damaged

Ending lease if property destroyed or damaged

Re-entry and forfeiture

Tenant's compensation on quitting

Landlord's right to use neighbouring land

Landlord's non-liability for accidents on the property

Notices

Dispute resolution

Goods left by tenant

No warranty on use

No waiver of covenants

Quiet enjoyment

Third part rights excluded

Release from landlord covenants on assignment of reversion

(b) Of course it may be necessary to depart from this in some circumstances.

(c) The assumptions that underlie a running order are:

(i) matters of substance, such as the price, the contract period and payment dates should appear early

(ii) procedural matters (notices, dispute resolution, insurance and the like) should go in the middle

(iii) default provisions (what happens if things go wrong) should come towards the end.

(d) Where a document contains an index of abbreviations or defined terms, the index would appear at the very end.

6.3 PROPER LAW AND THE FORUM FOR DISPUTES

In most instances where the subject-matter of the document is wholly within England and Wales (eg a lease of property within the jurisdiction) it will be unnecessary to consider the separate questions of the applicable law and the appropriate forum for resolving disputes. In contracts with an international element, it will be necessary to consider both points, and add a clause along the following lines—

This agreement is to be construed in accordance with the law of England and the forum for litigation is England

6.4 TERM

(a) Commencement

A contract or other document inter partes will normally come into effect once it is executed. If you want to delay its implementation in whole or in part, you should say so.

(b) Termination

You should also make clear when or in what circumstances the contract will come to an end, either automatically or on the happening of some event, eg after service of notice. Otherwise it could be held to last indefinitely, or at any rate the position will be unclear.

(c)   Leases

Remember than in leases there are three distinct dates, namely—

(i)   the date of the lease

(ii)   the beginning of the term

(iii)   the date the payment of rent starts.

These dates might well be all the same, or the term might begin before the date of the lease with no rent-free period. In any event you will have at least to consider these three dates and the often tricky relationship between them. For instance a rent-free period will usually begin on the date of the lease rather than on an earlier commencement of the term.

PART 7

PRECEDENTS-PRINCIPLES

7.1 USE OF PRECEDENTS

Precedents (otherwise forms or templates) are a necessary part of drafting private documents. Few of us are confident enough to begin with a blank sheet of paper. Yet precedents should be used with care and should never be adopted slavishly. In most firms, fee earners are responsible for the drafts they send out and for the form and effectiveness of the final document. So fee earners must tailor precedents to the job in hand.

7.2 THE DANGERS OF PRECEDENTS

(a) Remember that precedents (particularly those in books and from service providers) are usually written on an "all-risks / all possibilities" basis. In the majority of cases, they can be edited to suit the particular task, often radically.

(b) The power of the printed word is strong. So is a precedent produced for use in-house. It is often tempting to regard someone else's work as written in stone, never to be deviated from. But if circumstances demand it, a precedent must be varied.

(c) Precedent use probably accounts for the formulaic and unhelpful structure of many legal documents: that is, a long string of dictionary-type definitions at the beginning, the operative part in the middle and the nitty-gritty in schedules at the end. This is an explanation but should not be an excuse. Resist a structure of this kind, which is hard on any reader.

7.3 EXECUTION OF DEEDS

For the various forms of execution of deeds, see Land Registry Practice Guide 8 'Execution of deeds'.

7.4   STATUTORY MEANINGS IN PRIVATE DOCUMENTS

(a)   Introduction

The provisions of the Law of Property Act 1925 section 61 (construction of expressions used in deeds and other instruments) are well known, if not always applied. What is less well known (or maybe in some cases hardly known at all) are those parts of the Interpretation Act which affect private documents.

(b)   Law of Property Act 1925 section 61

(i)   This section provides that unless the context requires otherwise, in all private documents—

- "month" means calendar month
- "person" includes a corporation
- the singular includes the plural and vice versa
- the masculine includes the feminine and vice versa

(ii)   Confusingly in Acts of Parliament and the like, "person" includes an unincorporated body: see Interpretation Act 1978 section 5 and schedule 1. It's worth remembering that unless you extend the meaning in a private document, "person" will not include unincorporated bodies like members' clubs and business partnerships.

(c)   Interpretation Act 1978 section 23(3)

(i)   The subsection provides as follows.

"Sections 9 and 19(1) also apply to deeds and other instruments and documents as they apply to Acts and subordinate legislation; and in the application of section 17(2)(a) to Acts passed or subordinate legislation made after the commencement of this Act, the reference to any other enactment includes any deed or other instrument or document."

(d)   Section 9 of the Interpretation Act: the time of day

This says that references to the time of day mean Greenwich mean time or British Summer Time, depending on which is in effect. Nothing at all startling or unexpected in that.

(e)   Section 19(1) of the Interpretation Act: amended Acts etc

This subsection is itself not that easy to understand, but it seems to mean that references in Acts (and hence in private documents) to Acts and other public instruments are to be read as references to those Acts and other public instruments as amended from time to time.

If that is right there is strictly no need in private documents to make express provision to the same effect. But the drafter may wish to leave in any such express provisions, if only because sections 9 and 19(1) are so little known and their meaning is not entirely obvious.

(f)   Section 17(2)(a) of the Interpretation Act: re-enactments

(i)   This provides that references to an enactment which has been repealed and re-enacted are to the re-enactment. The comments above apply to this provision too.

(ii)   It follows that where you do not want this general rule to apply (eg in relation to the Town and Country Planning (Use Classes) Order 1987) you should say so explicitly.

PART 8

PLANS

8.1   THE NEED FOR ACCURATE PLANS

For property transactions, a plan is often needed. Wait for the plan before you begin drafting the document. A good plan will shorten the number of words you have to use, and will focus your mind on what you need to say.

8.2   PROFESSIONALLY-DRAWN PLANS

Solicitors should no more play at being plans drawers than they should play at being surveyors. Except in the most extreme of circumstances, get plans drawn professionally.

8.3   "FOR THE PURPOSE OF IDENTIFICATION ONLY"

These words are not acceptable to Land Registry, and they should not be acceptable to the parties or their lawyers. If a plan is used, it should be as accurate as the scale allows.

8.4   LAND REGISTRY PRACTICE

Land Registry practice on plans is set out in its Practice Guide 40. Supplement 2 of that guide sets out the detailed requirements. In essence:

(i)   use the scales 1 : 1250 or 1 : 500 for urban properties

(ii)   use the scale 1 : 2500 for fields, farms and the like

(iii)   show the location by roads, junctions or other landmarks

(iv)   identify different floor levels where appropriate

(v)   show the orientation (eg a north point).

8.5 SCALE ALTERATION

Be careful not to alter the scale inadvertently when copying a plan, eg by indicating 'fit to page' for your printer.

8.6 MARKINGS

Land Registry follows British conventions. These can be summarized like this.

Land of the subject of the documents (eg the property to be sold or let)	Red edging
Rights of way benefitting the property	Brown colouring or brown hatching
Rights of way to which the property is subject	Blue colouring or blue hatching
Drainage rights	Coloured broken line

You do not have to follow these conventions, but they generally help. However it is often clearer to tint the whole of the core property, usually in a colour close to red or pink.

8.7 EXAMPLE PLAN

There follows a plan which does not adhere to the BSI conventions, but which in context has been shown to do the job. Here:

Land the subject of the document (ie the let property)	Pink colouring
Vehicular right of way benefitting the property	Coloured blue hatched black
Rubbish area benefitting the property	Red colouring
Visitors' parking	Green colouring
Tenant's parking	Yellow colouring

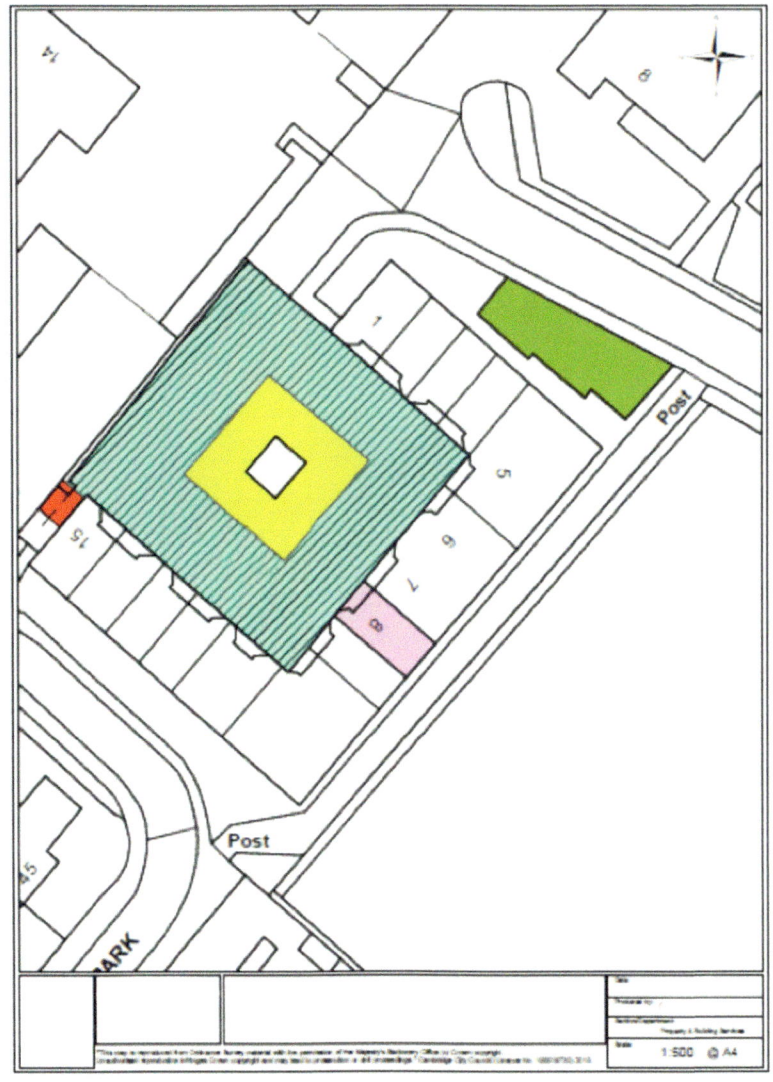

PART 9

"SUBJECT TO PLANNING PERMISSION"

An agreement to buy or lease land subject to the prospective buyer or tenant obtaining planning permission can be incredibly time-consuming to settle. The landowner looks for the certainty of a sale, whereas the would-be buyer only wants the property if he can get planning permission which is satisfactory to him. Numerous other issues swirl around. What if the planning permission is refused, or given late? What if an aggrieved neighbour goes for judicial review? Should the buyer appeal a refusal or an onerous condition? The result is often a mish-mash of overlapping qualifications, a leaping around from definition to definition and from definitions to operative clause, and a loss of the main aim and how the parties expect to achieve it. In short, most of the worst features of present-day legal documents in England are embodied in the contract: it is difficult to interpret, hard to read and easy for a disgruntled buyer to wriggle out of.

There must be a better way. Hence the following model form. Because time is expressed to be of the essence of the long-stop date, see the discussion on the corresponding date rule in para 5.7 ante. The model form tries to recognise the following fundamentals of the position.

1. The buyer must have control over whether or not a planning situation is satisfactory.

2. The landowner must be reassured that the buyer does not call all the shots.

3. Convoluted attempts to cover every single possibility (however remote) and give them all equal weight are counter-productive; and the chance that either party might assume a risk he is unaware of should be minimised.

True, a simple option might well do the job better. But sellers like the conditional contract because it can seem more certain – and hence more valuable.

THIS CONTRACT is made the   day of   202▶

BETWEEN

▶   of

▶ ("the Landlord"); and

▶   LIMITED company number ▶
whose registered office is at ▶

                        ("the Tenant").

1.   AGREEMENT TO LEASE

The Landlord will grant and the Tenant will take a lease of ▶
                                    ("the property") in the form of
lease attached to this contract ("the lease"). The property is more
particularly described in the lease.

2.   PRECONDITION ON GRANT OF LEASE.

2.1   The grant of the lease is conditional on the Tenant obtaining
satisfactory planning permission for ▶ [change of use of the
property to class B8 (storage or distribution) of the Town and
Country Planning (Use Classes) Order 1987.]

2.2   It is for the Tenant to decide on rational grounds whether or not a
planning permission is satisfactory.

2.3   The Tenant will submit its planning application within 28 days of
the date of this contract.

3.   COMPLETION

3.1   Completion of the lease will take place 14 days after the Tenant
notifies the Landlord that it has satisfactory planning permission
and is willing to proceed.

3.2   The Tenant will give that notification as soon as practicable. But
the Tenant may delay the notification to take account of—

(a)   a potential or actual application for judicial review of the
planning permission granted

(b)   a potential or actual application under section 288 of
the Town and Country Planning Act 1990 (proceedings
for questioning the validity of orders, decisions and
directions)

    (c)   negotiating and completing a planning agreement or unilateral undertaking under section 106 of the Town and Country Planning Act 1990

    (d)   pursuing a planning appeal, namely an appeal by the Tenant against—

            (i)   a refusal of planning permission

            (ii)   non-determination of a planning application, or

            (iii)   a condition attached to a planning permission; or

    (e)   submission of a fresh planning application by the Tenant.

4.   LONG-STOP DATE

This contract will cease to have effect if the lease has not been completed on the corresponding date ▶ [six months] after today ("the long-stop date"). Time is of the essence of the long-stop date.

5.   VACANT POSSESSSION

Vacant possession of the property will be granted on completion of the lease.

6.   GENERAL CONDITIONS

The Standard Commercial Property Conditions (third edition, 2018 revision) are incorporated in this contract. Where there is a difference between those conditions and this contract, this contract prevails.

7.   LEASE CLAUSES INCORPORATED

The provisions in the lease about notices, dispute resolution, and governing law and jurisdiction apply to this contract.

8.   SECURITY OF TENURE EXCLUDED

8.1   The Landlord and the Tenant agree that the provisions of sections 24 to 28 of the Landlord and Tenant Act 1954 (security of tenure) are excluded in relation to the tenancy to be created by the lease.

8.2   The Landlord has served the notice referred to in section 38A(3) (a) of that Act on the Tenant.

8.3   The Tenant has made a declaration or statutory declaration substantially in the form set out in schedule 2 to the Regulatory Reform (Business Tenancies) (England and Wales) Order 2003.

9. TITLE

The Landlord's title to the property has been deduced to the Tenant before the date of this contract.

10. NON-ASSIGNMENT

This contract is personal to the Tenant and the Tenant may not assign, charge, declare a trust over or deal in any other way with any of its rights and obligations under this contract.

11. TERMINATION FOR BREACH OR INSOLVENCY

Without affecting any other right or remedy available to it, the Landlord may terminate this contract with immediate effect by giving notice to the Tenant if—

11.1   the Tenant is in fundamental breach of any of it obligations in this contract; or

11.2   a forfeiting event within the meaning of the lease occurs.

12. CANCELLATION OF LAND REGISTRY ENTRIES

If this contract ceases to have effect, the Tenant will as soon as practicable apply to Land Registry to remove any entry in the Landlord's registered title that it may have caused to be made on account of this contract.

13. ENTIRE AGREEMENT

13.1   This contract constitutes the whole agreement between the parties. It supersedes all previous correspondence, negotiations, arrangements and agreements between them relating to its subject-matter.

13.2   The Tenant acknowledges that in entering into this contract the Tenant does not rely on any representation or warranty, whether made innocently or negligently.

13.3   Nothing in this clause limits or excludes liability for fraud.

EXECUTED AS A DEED   )

by affixing the common seal of   )

▶   )

in the presence of:)

Authorised officer

EXECUTED as a DEED by   )

▶   LIMITED   )

acting by a director in the presence of:)   ....

                                                Director

                                          ....

                                            Name of director (printed)

Witness signature ....……………

Name of witness (printed) ....….………..

Address ....………………….

.........................….…………………….

.........................….…………………….

Occupation ....………....…………….

OPTION AGREEMENT

The option agreement which follows is unusual in that it is made by deed (agreements under hand will usually suffice); it calls for a capital sum to be paid by the option holder as a precondition to exercise of the option (clause 2.2); and it provides for payment of overage (clause 7).

As with all option agreements, it is important to be clear on when action must happen. Valuable rights are lost if steps are taken out of time.

DATE: **202▶**

OPTION DEED

relating to

LAND AT ▶

THIS OPTION DEED is made the   day of   2020

BETWEEN

▶   ("the Landowner")

and

▶   company number▶   whose registered office is

at ▶

                                                            ("the Optionholder").

1.   GRANT OF OPTION

The Landowner grants to the Optionholder the right for the period of one year beginning on the date of this deed ("the option period") to take a lease of land at ▶   ("the Property") in the form of the draft lease attached to this deed ("the lease"). The Property is more particularly described in the lease.

2.   EXERCISE NOTICE AND PAYMENT OF PREMIUM

2.1   At any time during the option period the Optionholder may exercise the option by service on the Landowner of a notice substantially in the form set out in the schedule ("the option notice").

2.2   But the option notice is to be of no effect unless before service of it the Optionholder has paid the sum of ▶   pounds to the Landowner by transferring that sum to the following bank account:

▶

3.   CONDITIONS FOR GRANT OF LEASE

3.1   Evidence of the Landowner's title to the Property has already been provided to the Optionholder's solicitors.

3.2   The Standard Conditions of Sale (fourth edition) will apply, so far as consistent with the terms of this deed.

3.3   The Landowner will grant the lease one month from service of the option notice ("the completion date")

3.4   The Landowner will engross the lease and counterpart.

4. DISPOSALS

4.1 In the option period and except as envisaged in this deed, the Landowner will not dispose of a legal or equitable interest in the Property to a person other than the Optionholder.

4.2 The Optionholder may place a restriction on the register of the Landowner's title that during the option period no dealing may be registered without the Optionholder's consent.

4.3 The Optionholder may not assign the benefit of this deed.

5. NOTICES AND EXPIRY DATES

5.1 A notice, notification on payment under this deed may be given to or made by the party concerned or the solicitors for that party.

5.2 Where the completion date or the expiry date of a notice or of the option period falls on a day which is not a working day, the relevant date is to be the next working day. A notice or payment is effective only if given or made by 4pm on the day in question.

6. VALUE ADDED TAX

The Landowner confirms it has not opted to tax the Property for VAT purposes and will not do so before completion of the lease.

7. OVERAGE

7.1 **General rule**

(a) On the first arms-length assignment of the lease other than by way of mortgage or charge, the Optionholder will pay the Landowner 51.48% of the premium received by the Optionholder after allowing for all costs reasonably and properly incurred by the Optionholder in relation to the Property plus 17.5% profit on those costs.

(b) The Optionholder's costs under (a) are to be specified in a schedule accompanied by a certificate from a suitably-qualified independent chartered or certified accountant or surveyor. As soon as practicable after completion of the works, the Optionholder must serve those documents on the Landowner. If the parties are unable to agree the figure for the costs or the subsequent calculation under this clause, the matter is to be dealt with by the dispute resolution provisions of the lease.

7.2   **What is an arms-length assignment**

An assignment is not to be treated as being at arms-length if either it is to an associated company of the Optionholder or it is at less than open market value. Open market value is the figure for which this lease should be assigned at arms-length by a willing seller to a willing buyer after proper marketing, where the parties each act prudently, knowledgeably and without compulsion and on the basis of an assessment of the Property in accordance with RICS valuation standards then current.

7.3   **Payment if no arms-length assignment within three years**

(a)   If the Optionholder has made no arms-length assignment within three years of the date of first occupation under clause 4.1 of the lease (and time is of the essence of this stipulation) the Optionholder will pay to the Landowner a lump sum equivalent to what would have been payable at the end of those three years if there had been an arms-length assignment at that time.

(b)   The lump sum is to be treated as due at the end of the three-year period and accordingly bears interest at the rate stipulated for late payments under the lease.

SCHEDULE

Suggested form of exercise notice

To: ▶

Option deed dated ▶20 made between yourselves and ourselves ("the option deed") relating to land at ▶ ("the Property")

1. We refer to the option deed relating to the Property.

2. We give you notice that we have deposited £▶ in your bank account and we exercise our option to take a lease of the Property.

    SIGNED for the Optionholder

    …………………………………………………..

    Authorised to sign on behalf of the company

EXECUTED AS A DEED   )

by affixing the common seal of   )

)

in the presence of:)

Head of Legal Services

EXECUTED as a DEED by   )

The Optionholder   )

acting by its officers:)

Director

Company secretary/Director

HOUSE TRUST DEED

Although trust deeds like the one that follows are not confined to families, it is often the case that different parts or generations of the same family combine their resources to buy a property in which one or more of them intends to live.

This readily-adaptable precedent envisages the common situation where some participants have capital and others have borrowing-power. Although it envisages that one party will probably live at the property, it covers the position when none of them does (clause 8). It also deals with a situation where a party would like to sell his or her share, and provides for the sale of the property itself if the parties are not able to agree a price for the outgoing owner's proportion (clause 7).

THIS TRUST DEED is made the   day of   2020

BETWEEN:

▶   ("William and Mary")

▶   ("Olly")

▶   ("Jack and Jill")

1. Background

1.1 William and Mary are entitled to be registered as proprietors of the freehold house known as ▶   ("the property") title to which is registered at Land Registry under title number ▶. The price paid was £▶.

1.2 The property was acquired with the aid of a mortgage advance of £▶ from ▶   secured by a registered charge ("the mortgage") on the property. In addition William and Mary contributed £▶   ; Olly contributed £▶   ; and Jack and Jill contributed £▶.

1.3 The costs of acquisition were borne by the equitable owners in their equitable shares (see clause 4).

2. Equitable owners

The owners of the property in equity ("the equitable owners") are:

William and Mary jointly;

Olly; and

Jack and Jill jointly.

3. Mortgage repayments

3.1 Olly undertakes to make all payments due under the mortgage, and will indemnify William and Mary against the consequences of failure to make the payments. Olly will also observe the conditions of the mortgage so far as they are capable of compliance by an occupier of the property.

3.2 If Olly defaults in making mortgage payments so that William and Mary bear them, the same amounts as the missing mortgage payments are to be deducted from Olly's contribution of £▶ and added to William and Mary's contribution of £▶; and the equitable shares are to be adjusted accordingly.

4. Declaration of trust

William and Mary declare that they hold the property on trust for the equitable owners in the following equitable shares:

William and Mary ▶%

Olly ▶%

Jack and Jill ▶%.

5. **Purposes of the trust**

The purposes of the trust (in descending order of importance) are:

5.1 to provide a residence for Olly;

5.2 to be an investment for the equitable owners; and

5.3 to find a retirement dwelling for Jack and Jill.

6. **Obligations relating to the property**

6.1 An occupier of the property who is one of the equitable owners will—

(a) take care of it;

(b) insure it to its full replacement value;

(c) pay all outgoings, including council tax and payments for electricity, telephone, water, fuel oil, television, and internet supplies.

6.2 Such an occupier may also allow a lodger or other licensee to use part of the property temporarily on terms reasonably acceptable to the equitable occupier. In that event, and without affecting the obligation under the preceding subclause, the equitable occupier may keep the whole income from the licensee.

6.3 The equitable owners will pay for repairs and improvements to the property in their equitable shares.

7. **Disposal of equitable shares**

7.1 If any of the equitable owners wishes to dispose of the whole or part of his her or their equitable share, they must first offer it to the others. The value of the share is to be found by taking the relevant percentage of the net sale proceeds of the property, assuming a sale in the open market with vacant possession.

7.2 If the parties are unable to agree within one month of the offer either on the value of the outgoing equitable owner's share or part share, or on how it is to be distributed to the remaining equitable owners, the property is to be sold with vacant possession, and the net sale proceeds divided between the equitable owners according to their equitable shares at the time.

8. **Letting if not occupied by an equitable owner**

8.1 If none of the equitable owners wants to occupy the property and none of them wishes to sell it, the property is to be let in the open market on the best terms reasonably obtainable.

8.2 Olly remains liable to make mortgage payments in accordance with clause 3, and (subject to the provisions of that clause and to the rest of this deed) the equitable shares remain the same.

8.3 The equitable owners are entitled to the net income from the property in their equitable shares.

SIGNED AS A DEED by   )
)
in the presence of:)

Witness signature…………………………………...............

Witness name (printed)……………………….................

Witness address…………………………………….........

………………………………………………………........

Witness occupation…………………………….............

TRANSFER WITH OVERAGE

Overage is tricky and cannot be regarded as bombproof in all circumstances. The provisions of the transfer which follow envisage that the transferee might well try to escape from the confines of the overage.

This transfer only deals with a disposal for a use different from the current use. Accordingly it sets out the general rule (clause 17 (a)) and specifies the current use in full (clause 17 (d)). It also attempts to deal with disposal of part or parts of the property by the transferee (clause 17 (g)).

The form TP1 is Crown copyright and is reproduced with the permission of HM Land Registry under delegated authority from the controller of HMSO.

HM Land Registry
Transfer of part of registered title(s)

Any parts of the form that are not typed should be completed in black ink and in block capitals.

If you need more room than is provided for in a panel, and your software allows, you can expand any panel in the form. Alternatively use continuation sheet CS and attach it to this form.

For information on how HM Land Registry processes your personal information, see our Personal Information Charter.

Leave blank if not yet registered.	1	Title number(s) out of which the property is transferred: ▶
When application for registration is made these title number(s) should be entered in panel 2 of Form AP1.	2	Other title number(s) against which matters contained in this transfer are to be registered or noted, if any: NONE
Insert address, including postcode (if any), or other description of the property transferred. Any physical exclusions, such as mines and minerals, should be defined.	3	Property: ▶
Place 'X' in the appropriate box and complete the statement.		The property is identified
For example 'edged red'.		☒ on the attached plan and shown tinted pink:
For example 'edged and numbered 1 in blue'.		☐ on the title plan(s) of the above titles and shown:
Any plan lodged must be signed by the transferor.		
Remember to date this deed with the day of completion, but not before it has been signed and witnessed.	4	Date:
Give full name(s) of **all** of the persons transferring the property.	5	Transferor: ▶
Complete as appropriate where the transferor is a company.		For UK incorporated companies/LLPs Registered number of company or limited liability partnership including any prefix:
		For overseas companies (a) Territory of incorporation:
		(b) Registered number in the United Kingdom including any prefix:

81

Give full name(s) of **all** the persons to be shown as registered proprietors.	**6** Transferee for entry in the register: ▶ For UK incorporated companies/LLPs Registered number of company or limited liability partnership including any prefix: ▶
Complete as appropriate where the transferee is a company. Also, for an overseas company, unless an arrangement with HM Land Registry exists, lodge either a certificate in Form 7 in Schedule 3 to the Land Registration Rules 2003 or a certified copy of the constitution in English or Welsh, or other evidence permitted by rule 183 of the Land Registration Rules 2003.	For overseas companies (a) Territory of incorporation: (b) Registered number in the United Kingdom including any prefix:
Each transferee may give up to three addresses for service, one of which must be a postal address whether or not in the UK (including the postcode, if any). The others can be any combination of a postal address, a UK DX box number or an electronic address.	**7** Transferee's intended address(es) for service for entry in the register: ▶
	8 The transferor transfers the property to the transferee
Place 'X' in the appropriate box. State the currency unit if other than sterling. If none of the boxes apply, insert an appropriate memorandum in panel 12.	**9** Consideration ☒ The transferor has received from the transferee for the property the following sum (in words and figures): ▶ POUNDS(£▶) plus value added tax of ▶ pounds (£▶) ☐ The transfer is not for money or anything that has a monetary value ☐ Insert other receipt as appropriate:
Place 'X' in any box that applies. Add any modifications.	**10** The transferor transfers with ☒ full title guarantee ☐ limited title guarantee

82

Where the transferee is more than one person, place 'X' in the appropriate box.

11 Declaration of trust. The transferee is more than one person and

☐ they are to hold the property on trust for themselves as joint tenants

☐ they are to hold the property on trust for themselves as tenants in common in equal shares

Complete as necessary.

☐ they are to hold the property on trust:

The registrar will enter a Form A restriction in the register *unless*:
– an 'X' is placed:
   – in the first box, or
   – in the third box and the details of the trust or of the trust instrument show that the transferees are to hold the property on trust for themselves alone as joint tenants, *or*
– it is clear from completion of a form JO lodged with this application that the transferees are to hold the property on trust for themselves alone as joint tenants.

Please refer to *Joint property ownership* and *practice guide 24: private trusts of land* for further guidance. These are both available on the GOV.UK website.

Use this panel for:
– definitions of terms not defined above
– rights granted or reserved
– restrictive covenants
– other covenants
– agreements and declarations
– any required or permitted statements
– other agreed provisions.

The prescribed subheadings may be added to, amended, repositioned or omitted.

Any other land affected by rights granted or reserved or by restrictive covenants should be defined by reference to a plan.

12 Additional provisions

12.1 Definitions

NONE

Any other land affected should be defined by reference to a plan and the title numbers referred to in panel 2.

12.2 Rights granted for the benefit of the property

NONE

Any other land affected should be defined by reference to a plan and the title numbers referred to in panel 2.

12.3 Rights reserved for the benefit of other land

NONE

12.4 Restrictive covenants by the transferee

NONE

12.5 Restrictive covenants by the transferor

NONE

12.6 Recovery of part uplift amounts

(a) General rule

(i) On a disposition with a different use of the whole or part of the property in the period of 10 years beginning with and including the date of this transfer ("the overage period") the Transferee will pay the Transferor the prescribed proportion of the uplift amount. A 'disposition' is as defined in section 27(2) of the Land Registration Act 2002, except that for the purposes of this clause—
the grant of a legal charge over the whole of the property is not a disposition, but
the grant of any lease or tenancy is a disposition.
(ii) If the property is disposed of for the same use it had on the immediately preceding disposition, no payment is to be made under this clause.

(b) Prescribed proportion

The prescribed proportion is 50% for the first five years of the overage period and 25% for the second five years of the overage period.

(c) Uplift amount

The uplift amount is the increase over the base figure of whichever of the following is the higher:
(i) the amount realised on the disposition, and
(ii) the open market value of the property on the disposition.

(d) Base figure on first disposition

Subject to the following paragraphs, the base figure on a first disposition is the open market value of the property at the date of the disposition on the assumption that the property is disposed of for its current use. To avoid misunderstanding, its current use is—
use of the ground floor as and for a high class restaurant with kitchens and food preparation and storage areas and dining rooms for diners to eat on the premises; and (but only as ancillary to the main dining–in restaurant use) a takeaway facility for food to be consumed off the premises; and use of the first floor area for the above purposes or for residential accommodation for bona fide members of staff employed at the property (and their immediate families) upon the strict basis in each case of a bona fide employee's service occupancy agreement which shall contain provision for automatic termination on the date of termination of the employment of

84

such member of staff; and use of the basement and outbuildings of the property for storage purposes only ancillary to the main restaurant use.

(e) Base figure on subsequent dispositions

Subject to the following paragraphs, the base figure on second and subsequent dispositions is the open market value of the property at the date of the disposition on the assumption that the property is disposed of for the use it had on the immediately preceding disposition.

(f) 'Open market value'

References in this clause to open market value are to the estimated amount for which the property (or the relevant part) should exchange between a willing buyer and a willing seller in a transaction at arm's length after proper marketing, in which the parties had each acted knowledgeably, prudently and without compulsion; and on the basis that it is assessed in accordance with RICS valuation standards then current.

(g) Disposition of part

Where part only of the property is being disposed of, the base figure is a proper proportion of the base figure for the whole of the property, having regard to—
(i) the position of the part and the area (including the floor area) of the property it encompassed at the date of this transfer
(ii) best practice in valuation at the time of the disposition
(iii) professional guidelines on valuation available at the time of the disposition
(iv) the preceding paragraphs relating to base figures.

(h) Restriction on register

(i) The Transferor and the Transferee apply to the registrar for the entry of a restriction in the following form against the Transferee's title to the property, or in a form as near to it as the registrar will allow:
No disposition of the registered estate (other than a charge of the whole) by the proprietor of the registered estate, or by the proprietor of a charge not being a charge registered before the entry of this restriction, is to be registered without a written consent signed by ▶ .
(ii) As soon as practicable, the Transferee will supply the Transferor with evidence that the restriction has been entered.
(iii) At the end of the overage period and on the request of the Transferee, the Transferor will at its cost apply to the registrar to remove the restriction. The Transferee and its successors in title are free to assign the benefit of this covenant to a subsequent owner of the property.
(iv) The Transferor covenants with the Transferee and its successors in title not unreasonably to withhold or delay provision of the consent (or proper refusal of consent) referred to above. The Transferee and its successors in title are free to assign the benefit of this covenant to a subsequent owner of the property.

(i) Dispute resolution

(i) If the parties cannot agree on any question arising from this clause, it is to be referred to an independent surveyor.
(ii) Either party may apply at any time to the President of the

appointment of the independent surveyor.

(iii) If the appointed independent surveyor dies or becomes unwilling or incapable of acting then either party may apply to the President of the Royal Institution of Chartered Surveyors to discharge the appointed independent surveyor and to appoint a replacement.

(iv) The independent surveyor is to act as an expert and is to give a written copy of his or her decision to both parties within 20 working days after the date of the independent surveyor's appointment. The decision may include the award of interest. If the dispute relates to the interpretation of a provision in this transfer, the surveyor may seek advice from an independent solicitor or barrister.

(v) The parties are each entitled to make submissions to the independent surveyor and must provide (or procure that others provide) the independent surveyor with the assistance and documents that the independent surveyor reasonably requires to reach a decision.

(vi) The independent surveyor's written decision is final and binding in the absence of manifest error or fraud.

(vii) The independent surveyor is free to make an award of cost as he or she directs. In the absence of a direction, each party is to bear its own costs and the independent surveyor's costs are to be borne by the parties equally.

The transferor must execute this transfer as a deed using the space opposite. If there is more than one transferor, all must execute. Forms of execution are given in Schedule 9 to the Land Registration Rules 2003. If the transfer contains transferee's covenants or declarations or contains an application by the transferee (such as for a restriction), it must also be executed by the transferee.

If there is more than one transferee and panel 11 has been completed, each transferee must also execute this transfer to comply with the requirements in section 53(1)(b) of the Law of Property Act 1925 relating to the declaration of a trust of land. Please refer to *Joint property ownership* and *practice guide 24: private trusts of land* for further guidance.

Examples of the correct form of execution are set out in *practice guide 8: execution of deeds*. Execution as a deed usually means that a witness must also sign, and add their name and address.

Remember to date this deed in panel 4.

13   Execution

EXECUTED as a DEED   )
by affixing the common seal of)
▶   )

in the presence of:

....
Signature of Director

....
Signature of [Director] [Secretary]

EXECUTED AS A DEED by   )
▶   )
acting by [a director and its   )
secretary] [two directors]:   )

....
Director

....
Company Secretary/Director

WARNING

If you dishonestly enter information or make a statement that you know is, or might be, untrue or misleading, and intend by doing so to make a gain for yourself or another person, or to cause loss or the risk of loss to another person, you may commit the offence of fraud under section 1 of the Fraud Act 2006, the maximum penalty for which is 10 years' imprisonment or an unlimited fine, or both.

Failure to complete this form with proper care may result in a loss of protection under the Land Registration Act 2002 if, as a result, a mistake is made in the register.

Under section 66 of the Land Registration Act 2002 most documents (including this form) kept by the registrar relating to an application to the registrar or referred to in the register are open to public inspection and copying. If you believe a document contains prejudicial information, you may apply for that part of the document to be made exempt using Form EX1, under rule 136 of the Land Registration Rules 2003.

© Crown copyright (ref: LR/HO) 06/19

86

COMMERCIAL LEASE

This all-purpose business lease is adaptable for a shop, office, food-takeaway or the like. The landlord maintains the structure (clause 10) and insures it (clause 12.1). The tenant reimburses the landlord for the insurance premium and pays all outgoings. The tenant maintains the interior and perhaps other parts such as the shopfront (clause 9). There is a rent review clause to open market value (clause 5). Forms of rent deposit agreement and authorised guarantee agreement are given in schedules 3 and 4 respectively.

The Land Registry prescribed clauses LR1 to LR14 are part of the lease and should be integrated in it: see the Land Registration (Amendment) (No 2) Rules 2005: SI No. 1982 of 2005. The prescribed clauses should not be treated as a kind of notice to be tacked on the front.

DATE: 20▶

▶ [*Insert name of landlord*]

and

▶ [*Insert name of tenant*]

and

▶ [*insert name of guarantor*]

LEASE

of

▶[*Address*]

LR1. Date of lease	
LR2. Title number(s)	**LR2.1 Landlord's title number(s)** ▶ **LR2.2 Other title numbers** NONE
LR3. Parties to this lease *Give full names, addresses and company's registered number, if any, of each of the parties. For Scottish companies use a SC prefix and for limited liability partnerships use an OC prefix. For foreign companies give territory in which incorporated.*	**Landlord** ▶ **Tenant** ▶ **Guarantor** ▶
LR4. Property	**In the case of a conflict between this clause and the remainder of this lease then, for the purposes of registration, this clause shall prevail.** ▶ [Short description] ▶ [tinted pink and pink hatched red] on the attached plan
LR5. Prescribed statements etc	NONE
LR6. Term for which the Property is leased	The term is as follows: the period of ▶ [fifteen] years beginning on ▶ [insert date]
LR7. Premium	NONE
LR8. Prohibitions or restrictions on disposing of this lease	This lease contains a provision that prohibits or restricts dispositions.
LR9. Rights of acquisition etc	**LR9.1 Tenant's contractual rights to renew this lease, to acquire the reversion or another lease of the Property, or to acquire an interest in other land** NONE **LR9.2 Tenant's covenant to (or offer to) surrender this lease** NONE **LR9.3 Landlord's contractual rights to acquire this lease** NONE

LR10. Restrictive covenants given in this lease by the Landlord in respect of land other than the Property	NONE
LR11. Easements	**LR11.1 Easements granted by this lease for the benefit of the Property** SCHEDULE 1 **LR11.2 Easements granted or reserved by this lease over the Property for the benefit of other property** SCHEDULE 2
LR12. Estate rentcharge burdening the Property	NONE
LR13. Application for standard form of restriction	NONE
LR14. Declaration of trust where there is more than one person comprising the Tenant *If the Tenant is one person, omit or delete all the alternative statements.* *If the Tenant is more than one person, complete this clause by omitting or deleting all inapplicable alternative statements.*	The Tenant is more than one person. They are to hold the Property on trust for themselves as joint tenants. OR The Tenant is more than one person. They are to hold the Property on trust for themselves as tenants in common in equal shares. OR The Tenant is more than one person. They are to hold the Property on trust Complete as necessary

1. DEFINITIONS

1.1 Clauses LR 1 to LR 14 contain some definitions, descriptions and explanations of words used in this lease. "The Property" is defined in clause LR 4 and "the term" is defined in clause LR 6. In addition, the following apply.

1.2 "The insured risks" are fire and such other risks as the Landlord may from time to time consider it desirable to insure against

1.3 The expressions "landlord covenant" "tenant covenant" and "authorised guarantee agreement" have the same meanings as in the Landlord and Tenant (Covenants) Act 1995.

2. INTERPRETATION

2.1 Gender and number

Words of one gender include any other gender, and the singular includes the plural and vice versa.

2.2 Joint and several benefit and liability

Where a party consists of more than one person, the rights and obligations of that party under this lease are rights and obligations of those persons separately, all together or in any combination.

2.3 Corporations

A person includes a company or other body corporate.

2.4 Obligations

A Tenant's obligation not to do anything includes an obligation not to allow that thing to be done by another person.

2.5 Amendment or repeal of statutes

(a) Reference to a repealed Act of Parliament is a reference to the Act which, with or without modification, replaces or corresponds to the repealed Act.

(b) Reference to an Act of Parliament which has been amended is a reference to that Act as amended.

(c) This subclause does not apply to the Town and Country Planning (Use Classes) Order 1987.

3.   **LETTING**

The Landlord lets the Property to the Tenant for the term with the rights specified in schedule 1, but retaining the rights set out in schedule 2.

4.   **RENT AND OTHER PAYMENTS BY TENANT**

4.1   **Amount of rent**

The rent is—

(a)   for the first ▶[five] years of the term, £▶ a year ▶[subject to the following subclause].

(b)   for the ▶ [second and third] ▶[five] years of the term, the figures found in accordance with clause 5.

4.2   **Payment of rent**

(a)   The Tenant promises to pay the rent to the Landlord without deduction or set-off by equal instalments in advance on ▶ [the first day of every month] [the usual quarter days, namely 25 March, 24 June, 29 September and 25 December].

(b)   The first payment is due on ▶ [the date of this lease] ▶[for the period starting with the beginning of the term and ending on the payment day following the date of this lease]. ▶ [No rent is payable for the first [three] months of the term.]

(c)   The rent must be paid by direct debit.

(d)   If payment starts or ends partway through a payment period, the rent will be apportioned.

(e)   The rent is exclusive of rates and other outgoings.

4.3   **Rates and other outgoings**

(a)   The Tenant must pay all business rates, taxes and outgoings that are now or may at any time during the term be charged, assessed or imposed upon the Property or upon the owner or occupier of it, excluding any payable by the Landlord on rent received or on a dealing with this lease or arising from the Landlord's ownership of the freehold of the Property. Subject to the next paragraph, the Tenant must pay the appropriate authority direct.

(b)   Where rates, taxes or other outgoings are assessed by reference to the Property jointly with other premises, the Tenant must pay to the Landlord the proportion reasonably attributed to the Property by the Landlord.

(c)   The Tenant must pay all value added tax that may from time to time be charged on the rent or other sums payable by the Tenant under this lease.

4.4   Insurance premiums

The Tenant must repay to the Landlord on demand the cost incurred by the Landlord from time to time in paying premiums to effect or maintain insurance of the Property in accordance with this lease. Where a premium is assessed by reference to the Property together with other premises, the Tenant must pay the proportion reasonably attributed to the Property by the Landlord.

4.5   Charges for gas, electricity and other supplies

Subject to clause 4.3(b) the Tenant must pay to the suppliers all charges (including meter and appliance rentals) for gas, electricity, water, telephone and other services to the Property, and promises to observe all present and future requirements of the supply companies.

4.6   Interest on late payment of sums due to the Landlord

If the Tenant fails to pay the rent or any other sum due under this lease within14 days of the due date, the Tenant must pay to the Landlord interest on the amount owing (at the rate of 4% above the base rate of the Landlord's bank for the time being) from the date when it was due to the date on which it is actually paid.

4.7   Costs of service of notices

The Tenant must pay on demand all expenses (including solicitors' costs and surveyors' fees) incurred by the Landlord which arise from, or aro incidontal to ▶

(a)   the preparation and service of a notice under section 146 of the Law of Property Act 1925

(b)   the contemplation or taking of proceedings under sections 146 and 147 of that Act whatever the outcome of those proceedings, and

(c)   the preparation and service of notices and schedules relating to repair of the Property, whether served before or within 9 months of the ending of this lease.

4.8 Shared facilities

The Tenant agrees to contribute a reasonable and proper proportion of the expense of repairing, maintaining and cleaning all party walls and all sewers, drains and other things used by the occupier of the Property in common with occupiers of premises adjoining or nearby.

4.9 Payments treated as rent

All payments due from the Tenant to the Landlord under this lease are to be treated as rent.

5. RENT REVIEW

5.1 Review dates

The rent is to be reviewed on the ▶ [fifth, tenth and fifteenth] anniversaries of the beginning of the term; and "review period" means the ▶ [second, the third or the fourth] ▶ [five] years of the term▶ [, as appropriate].

5.2 Ratchet provision

For ▶ [any] [the] review period, the revised rent is to be whichever is the greater of—

(a)   the new rent ascertained in accordance with this clause, and

(b)   the rent payable immediately beforehand.

5.3 Procedure

(a)   The new rent for a review period may be agreed at any time between the Landlord and the Tenant.

(b)   In the absence of agreement and not more than 6 months before the end of the [relevant] ▶ [five] years of the term, the Landlord may opt to have the new rent fixed either by an arbitrator or a valuer.

(c)   An arbitrator must act under the Arbitration Act 1996, and a valuer must act as an expert and not as an arbitrator.

(d)   The Landlord may apply to the President of the Royal Institution of Chartered Surveyors for the nomination of an arbitrator or a valuer.

5.4   **Principles for fixing new rent**

(a)   <u>Market rent</u>

The new rent is to be the yearly rent at which the Property might reasonably be expected to be let at the relevant review date, with the assumptions set out in (b) but disregarding the matters set out in (c).

(b)   <u>Assumptions</u>

The assumptions are that—

- the Property is available to let on the open market without a premium with vacant possession by a willing landlord to a willing tenant

- the term of the notional letting is ▶[five] years

- the Property is to be let as a whole and subject to the provisions of this lease other than the amount of rent but including the provisions for rent review

- the Property is fit and available for immediate occupation

- the Property may be used for any purpose allowed by this lease as varied or extended by any licence

- the covenants on the part of the Landlord and the Tenant have been fully observed

- no work has been carried out to the Property which has diminished the rental value

- if the Property has been destroyed or damaged, it has been fully restored

- no reduction is to be made to take account of any rental concession which on a new letting with vacant possession might be granted to the incoming tenant for fitting out.

(c)   <u>Disregards</u>

The matters to be disregarded are:

- any effect on rent of the fact that the Tenant, his subtenant or their predecessors in title have been in occupation of the Property

- any goodwill attached to the Property through the carrying on there of the business of the Tenant or his subtenant or their predecessors in title to their businesses

- any increase in value due to disregardable improvements to the Property.

(d) Disregardable improvements

To be disregardable, an improvement must have been carried out—

- with the consent of the Landlord where that consent is required, and

- by the Tenant or its subtenant or any of their predecessors in title during the term, and

- not pursuant to an obligation to the Landlord or to an obligation to comply with statute, or direction of a local authority, statutory body or body acting under royal charter.

5.5 Valuation

(a) The costs of nomination and the fees and expenses of any valuer are to be borne equally by the Landlord and the Tenant, who must otherwise bear their own costs.

(b) The valuer must allow the Landlord and the Tenant an opportunity to make representations to him.

5.6 Replacement of arbitrator or valuer

The President of the Royal Institution of Chartered Surveyors on the application of either the Landlord or the Tenant may discharge any arbitrator or valuer and appoint another in his place if—

(a) the arbitrator or valuer dies, delays, becomes unwilling, becomes unfit or becomes incapable of acting; or

(b) for any other reason the President considers the arbitrator or valuer ought to be replaced.

5.7 Memorandum of rent review

(a) When the amount of any revised rent has been agreed or fixed, the Landlord and the Tenant will sign memoranda of rent review and keep them with this lease and the counterpart.

(b)   The Landlord and the Tenant will bear their own costs of those memoranda.

5.8   **Interim payments of rent**

(a)   If the revised rent has not been agreed or fixed by the beginning of the review period, the Tenant must continue to pay rent at the rate previously payable.

(b)   On the date the revised rent is agreed or fixed the Tenant must pay the Landlord any shortfall between the rent agreed or fixed and the rent actually paid, together with interest on any shortfall.

(c)   The interest is payable at 2% above the base lending rate of the Landlord's bank, calculated on a day-to-day basis beginning with the relevant review date and ending on the date of actual payment of any shortfall (both days inclusive).

(d)   Any shortfall and interest is recoverable in the same way as rent in arrears.

5.9   **Failure to pay arbitrator or valuer**

(a)   This clause applies if either the Landlord or the Tenant fails to pay within 21 days of demand any costs or fees awarded against it or him by an arbitrator, or half the fees and expenses of a valuer.

(b)   The party not in default may pay the arbitrator or the valuer, and may then recover that payment from the party chargeable.

6.   USE OF THE PROPERTY

6.1   **Principal and subsidiary uses**

The Tenant may use the Property ▶ [for] [as follows]:

[▶(a)   the ground floor for the supply of takeaway food for consumption off the Property, together with ancillary consumption on the Property;

(b)   the basement for food preparation and storage in connection with the activity carried out on the ground floor; and

(c)   the yard for storage, access and car parking and for any other use ancillary to the above.]

6.2 Prohibition on other uses

The Tenant must not use the Property for any other purpose. But with the consent of the Landlord (not to be unreasonably withheld or delayed) the Tenant may change the use of the Property to any other use which falls within class ▶ A1 [A2] [A3] of the schedule to the Town and Country Planning (Use Classes) Order 1987. It will be reasonable for the Landlord to withhold its consent where the Landlord reasonably considers that the proposed use—

(a)   would compete excessively with any other trade or business within the terrace, group of shops or shopping centre of which the Property is part at the time of the request, or

(b)   is not in keeping with the nature of the Property or the terrace, group of shops or shopping centre, or

(c)   is not in accordance with the principles of good estate management, or

(d)   would or might constitute breach of a tenant covenant in this lease.

6.3 Keep open for trade

The Tenant must remain open for trade during the usual shopping hours for the class of business carried on by the Tenant. The Tenant is not required to keep open for trade in any period during which—

(a)   the Tenant is carrying out authorised fitting-out works or other alterations

(b)   it is not possible to occupy the Property following damage or destruction by an insured risk, or

(c)   occupation or trading would result in breach of another provision of this lease.

6.4 Further restrictions on use of the Property

Specifically, the Tenant must not use the Property—

(a)   as sleeping accommodation or for a residential purpose

(b)   as a sex shop

(c)   for the sale of material which in the unfettered opinion of the Landlord is obscene, pornographic or indecent

(d) for the sale of sex aids, including pharmaceutical products and written materials

(e) in a way which may be a nuisance, disturbance, inconvenience or damaging to the Landlord or its tenants, or to owners or occupiers of neighbouring premises

(f) for a dangerous, radioactive, noxious, noisy or offensive trade, business or occupation

(g) as a licensed betting office

(h) for an illegal or immoral act or purpose

(i) for a sale by auction

(j) for the sale of intoxicating liquor, whether for consumption on or off the Property.

6.5 **Dangerous materials**

The Tenant must not bring on to or store at the Property any article, substance or liquid of a specially combustible, inflammable radioactive or dangerous nature.

6.6 **Nuisance notice**

If the Landlord gives notice to the Tenant requiring the stopping of a nuisance caused by vibration, noise or offensive smell, or by undue emissions of smoke, gas, fumes, vapour or dust, the Tenant must stop the nuisance immediately.

6.7 **Obstruction of highway**

The Tenant must not place any goods, machine, caseboard, sign or other material near the Property or in the adjacent highway, or obstruct the highway in any way.

6.8 **Encroachment and acquisition of rights**

(a) The Tenant must take all reasonable steps to prevent a trespass upon the Property or the acquisition of any new right to light, right of way, right of drainage or other easement over, on or under the Property.

(b) The Tenant must give notice to the Landlord of any threatened trespass or attempt to acquire an easement or right of the kind referred to above as soon as the Tenant becomes aware of it.

(c) If requested by the Landlord, the Tenant must stop the trespass, acquisition of an easement or right of that kind.

(d)   The Tenant must allow the Landlord (on reasonable notice except in an emergency) to enter the Property to do anything necessary to prevent an encroachment or acquisition of an easement or right.

6.9   Discharge into pipes and drains

(a)   The Tenant must not discharge any oil, grease, acid or other noxious, toxic or corrosive substance into any pipe or drain serving the Property—

- which may cause an obstruction in, or damage to, any such pipe or drain; or

- to which any water or sewerage company or other competent authority may object.

(b)   If any discharge occurs, the Tenant must immediately—

- make good any obstruction or damage to the satisfaction of the Landlord and the water or sewerage company or other competent authority; and

- comply with the reasonable requirements of the Landlord and the water or sewerage company or other competent authority to remedy the discharge or passage or to prevent its recurrence.

6.10   Overloading floors

The Tenant must not overload the floors of the Property.

6.11   Display of advertisements

Except as part of a normal window display, the Tenant must not (without the consent of the Landlord) display notices, posters or advertisements of any type whatsoever on the exterior of the Property or in the windows or doors of the Property. However, the Tenant may display a trade sign indicating the Tenant's name and a description of the Tenant's business on the external wall. The form, character and dimensions of the sign are subject to prior approval by the Landlord in writing.

6.12   Masts and wires

The Tenant must not erect any pole, mast or aerial or fix any cable or wire on the Property or install any equipment on it (whether or not in connection with telecommunications). This does not apply to an alarm for the security of the Property.

6.13   **Use affecting insurance policies**

(a)   The Tenant must not do anything on the Property which might invalidate any insurance policy taken out by the Landlord in respect of the Property, or in respect of any adjoining or neighbouring premises of the Landlord, or which might cause an increase in the premium charged for that insurance. The Tenant must repay to the Landlord all proper sums paid by the Landlord as a direct or indirect result of a breach of this covenant by the Tenant.

(b)   The Tenant must notify the Landlord as soon as the Tenant becomes aware of damage to the Property caused by an insured risk.

(c)   If at any time in the term the Property is damaged or destroyed by an insured risk through an act or default of the Tenant or the Tenant's employees, agents or visitors, and as a result the insurance money under an insurance policy taken out by the Landlord becomes irrecoverable, the Tenant must immediately pay to the Landlord the whole cost of completely rebuilding and reinstating the Property or (as the case may be) the proportion of that cost which is irrecoverable from the Landlord's insurers.

6.14   **Storage of refuse and waste**

The Tenant must store or deposit all waste or refuse in a proper covered receptacle on the Property.

6.15   **Stopping up windows**

The Tenant must not stop up, darken or obstruct a window or other aperture in the Property.

6.16   **Damage or injury arising from the Tenant's use of the Property**

The Tenant must protect (that is, indemnify) the Landlord against all losses, claims and expense arising directly or indirectly from—

(a)   the Tenant's use and occupation of the Property

(b)   an act, omission, negligence or default of the Tenant (or of the employees, agents, licensees or visitors of the Tenant), or

(c)   a breach by the Tenant of any of the terms of this lease.

6.17   **Fire precautions**

The Tenant must comply with all recommendations, requirements and directions of the Landlord, the competent fire authority and the Landlord's insurers about fire precautions for the Property and the means of escape in case of fire. The Tenant must ensure that the means of escape can be safely and effectively used at all times.

6.18   **Notices affecting the Property**

If the Tenant receives a communication from a competent authority affecting or likely to affect the Property, the Tenant must—

(a)   immediately send details to the Landlord

(b)   without delay, take all reasonable steps to comply with the communication at the Tenant's expense, and

(c)   join with the Landlord in making any representation to the communicating authority reasonably required by the Landlord.

6.19   **Electrics inspection**

The Tenant must arrange a periodic inspection of the electrical installations by an electrician approved by NICEIC, and provide the Landlord with a copy of the inspection report carried out in the last six months of the term (however it may end) ensuring that the electrician has undertaken the works required to enable the installations to pass as satisfactory.

6.20   **Gas servicing**

In the last twelve months of the term (however it may end) the Tenant must arrange a service of the gas boiler and gas installations (if any) by an engineer on the Gas Safe Register, and provide the Landlord with a certificate of safety.

7.   **PLANNING REQUIREMENTS**

7.1   **Breach of planning control**

The Tenant must not commit a breach of planning control.

7.2   **Application for planning consent**

(a)   Except with the written consent of the Landlord, the Tenant must not apply for planning permission to carry out any development at the Property or for change of use of the Property.

(b)   The Landlord may not unreasonably withhold its consent to apply for planning permission but it will always be reasonable for the Landlord to withhold consent if—

- the grant of the planning permission would have adverse implications for the Landlord, or

- grant of the planning permission might prejudice the restrictions on use in this lease.

(c)   In any event, the Tenant must supply the Landlord with—

- a copy of any application for planning permission

- a copy of any plans and other documents which the Landlord may reasonably require, and

- a copy of any planning permission granted to the Tenant.

7.3   **Charge on breach of planning control**

The Tenant must pay and satisfy any charge that may be imposed on breach by the Tenant of planning control or otherwise under the Town and Country Planning Act 1990.

7.4   **Works required by planning consent**

(a)   Unless the Landlord directs otherwise, the Tenant must carry out during the term works to the Property required as a condition of any planning permission granted during the term.

(b)   This applies whatever the date by which the works were stipulated to be carried out in the planning permission.

8.   **DEALINGS**

8.1   **General prohibition**

(a)   Except as provided in this clause, the Tenant may not deal with this lease, or part with or share possession or occupation of the Property or any part of it.

(b)   To "deal with" includes to assign, charge or underlet in whole or in part, and to hold on trust for another; and "dealing" is to be interpreted accordingly.

(c)   Provided no landlord and tenant relationship is established, sharing the whole or part of the Property with a company that is a member of the same group as the Tenant within section 42 of the Landlord and Tenant Act 1954 is not a breach of this clause.

8.2   **Assignment of whole**

(a)   General rule

The Tenant may assign the Property as a whole if the Tenant first—

- obtains the written consent of the Landlord in the form of a licence to assign under seal (and that licence is not to be unreasonably withheld)
- satisfies the circumstances referred to in (b), and
- complies with the conditions set out in (c).

The circumstances and conditions are prescribed for the purposes of the Landlord and Tenant Act 1927 section 19(1A).

(b)   Circumstances

The circumstances referred to are:

- all sums due from the Tenant under this lease must be paid up to the date of the assignment
- in the reasonable opinion of the Landlord, there must be no material breaches of any of the tenant covenants in this lease at the date of application for licence to assign
- in the reasonable opinion of the Landlord, the proposed assignee must be a person who is likely to be able to comply with the tenant covenants in this lease and to continue to be able to comply with them after the assignment.

(c)   Conditions

The conditions referred to are:

- if reasonably required by the Landlord, a rent deposit equivalent to up to six months rent must be paid to the Landlord, and the assignee will enter into a rent deposit agreement substantially in the form set out in schedule 3
- if reasonably required by the Landlord, before the assignment and before giving occupation to the assignee, the outgoing Tenant must enter into an authorised guarantee agreement substantially in the form set out in schedule 4

- if reasonably required by the Landlord on assignment to a company, the assignee must ensure that at least two directors of the company or some other guarantor or guarantors reasonably acceptable to the Landlord enter into direct covenants with the Landlord in the form of guarantor's covenants contained in this lease

- on completion of the licence to assign, the outgoing tenant or the assignee must pay the Landlord's reasonable legal costs and surveyors' fees incurred in preparation of the licence to assign and associated documents.

[▶8.3   Subletting of whole

(a)   General rule

The Tenant may sublet the Property as a whole if the Tenant first—

- obtains the written consent of the Landlord in the form of a licence to sublet under seal (and that licence is not to be unreasonably withheld)

- obtains a direct covenant by the subtenant with the Landlord to observe all the tenant covenants and other provisions of this lease (except the covenant to pay the reserved rent) and of the sublease

- if the Landlord reasonably requires, obtains an acceptable guarantor for the subtenant who must execute a deed containing direct covenants by the guarantor (or joint and several covenants if there is more than one guarantor) in terms reasonably required by the Landlord

- excludes sections 24 to 28 of the Landlord and Tenant Act 1954 from the subtenancy in accordance with section 38A of that Act

- pays the Landlord's reasonable legal costs and surveyors' fees in connection with the licence to sublet

- complies with the requirements for the sublease set out in paragraph (b).

(b)   Requirements for sublease

The sublease must—

- be granted at the market rent without a premium

- contain the same provisions as in this lease, except for any necessary changes and any amendments approved in writing by the Landlord

- contain a covenant by the subtenant not to do anything in relation to the Property inconsistent with the provisions of this lease

- contain a covenant by the subtenant to observe all the tenant covenants and other provisions of this lease (except the covenant to pay the reserved rent)

- contain a condition for re-entry on breach of covenant by the subtenant

- contain a clause recording the agreement of the Tenant (as landlord in the sublease) and the subtenant (as tenant in the sublease) that the provisions of sections 24 to 28 of the Landlord and Tenant Act 1954 are excluded in relation to the sublease

- contain provisions for review of the rent reserved by the sublease on the basis set out in this lease, including a ratchet clause

- provide that the subtenant has no right to deal with (see above) or part with or share possession of the whole or part of the Property.]

8.4   **Registration of dealings**

Within one month of a dealing with the Property, the Tenant must—

(a)   give notice of it to the Landlord and pay the Landlord's reasonable charges for registration of each dealing, and

(b)   send the Landlord a copy of the document by which the dealing was carried out.

9. MAINTENANCE, REPAIR AND ALTERATION: TENANT

9.1 Maintaining the Property

The Tenant must put and keep the ▶ [whole] [following parts of] the Property in repair and good condition (damage by the insured risks excepted) ▶[including]—

▶[(a)   the shop front and fascia]

(b)   all plaster-work, tiles, wallpaper and other wall coverings to all walls

(c)   all ceilings, plaster boards and other ceiling finishes

(d)   all floors and floor-boards, paving tiles, carpets and other floor finishes and floor coverings

(e)   all doors and door frames, windows and window frames (including locks, latches and fasteners) and all glass in windows and doors

(f)   the toilet facilities and the water, sanitary and heating apparatus and all sewers and drains and water and gas pipes and mains within the Property and serving it exclusively

(g)   the light fittings and other electrical fittings and all electricity cables, mains and wiring within the Property and serving it exclusively

(h)   all additions and improvements to the Property and all fixtures and fittings except fixtures belonging to the Tenant which can be removed without damage to the Property, and

▶[(i)   the boundary structures marked with an inward-facing T on the attached plan.]

9.2 Decorating the interior

(a)   To preserve the Property and to maintain a high standard of decorative finish and attractiveness, the Tenant must—

•   clean, prepare and paint in a workmanlike manner (with two coats of appropriate good quality paint) all the walls, woodwork, metal work and other parts of the interior of the Property previously or usually painted; and, with every such painting,

- varnish, emulsion, wash, stop, whiten and colour in a proper manner all parts which are usually dealt with in that way.

(b)   This obligation must be carried out as often as the Landlord reasonably considers necessary—

- but not more than once in any three year period, though

- in any event in every fifth year of the term and in the last year of the term however it ends.

9.3   **Decorating the exterior**

In a similar way and also in every fifth year of the term and in the last year (however it ends) the Tenant must decorate the exterior of the Property.

9.4   **Notice and entry to repair**

(a)   Within twenty-eight days from the date of a notice given by the Landlord (or sooner if the nature of the works requires it) the Tenant must carry out all works for which the Tenant is liable under this lease and which are referred to in the notice.

(b)   If within twenty-eight days of that notice the Tenant does not start and diligently carry out the works, then the Tenant must allow the Landlord, its employees or agents and others authorised by the Landlord to enter the Property and carry out the works. The Tenant must pay the whole cost of the works to the Landlord within fourteen days of a demand.

9.5   **Works and consents required by law and compliance with statutory directions**

(a)   The Tenant must comply with all statutes, regulations, orders, statutory instruments and byelaws whether made before or after the date of this lease and with all lawful directions and requirements of any local or public authority in respect of the Property or the Tenant's occupation or use of the Property.

(b)   The Tenant must carry out all works required in respect of the Property by or under statutes, regulations, orders, statutory instruments and byelaws whether made before or after the date of this lease.

(c)   The Tenant must obtain all approvals, consents and permissions (including planning permission) required by law in respect of the Property or the Tenant's use of the Property.

9.6   **Alterations and additions to the Property**

(a)   The Tenant must not make an alteration or addition to the Property without first obtaining—

- the consent of the Landlord in its role as landlord as opposed to its function as local or planning authority (and that consent may be granted or withheld at the discretion of the Landlord) and

- any planning permission or building consent which may be required.

(b)   The Tenant must comply with all conditions of those permissions and consents to the reasonable satisfaction of the Landlord.

(c)   Before vacating the Property the Tenant must (unless expressly released from this obligation) remove all alterations or additions and reinstate the Property to the satisfaction of the Landlord.

9.7   **Damage**

The Tenant must not cut, remove, alter or otherwise damage the Property, or any of the ceilings, walls, floors, girders, beams or timbers of the Property, or wires, pipes, drains, fixtures, or fittings of the Property.

9.8   **Condition of the Property at the end of the lease**

▶[(a)] At the end of the term the Tenant must vacate the Property and hand it back to the Landlord together with all fixtures (tenant's fixtures excepted) in repair and good condition, and decorated in accordance with this lease.

▶[(b)   But nothing in this lease obliges the Tenant to put or keep the Property in a condition better than the one it is now in as evidenced by the schedule of condition attached.]

▶[10.   **MAINTENANCE AND REPAIR OF STRUCTURE: LANDLORD**

10.1   The Landlord will maintain, repair and keep in good order and condition the main structure of the Property including the foundations, load bearing walls and the roof; and the tiles, slates or other roof coverings.

10.2   This obligation does not require the Landlord to carry out work—

(a)   called for as a result of the Tenant's negligence or default, or of the negligence or default of another person on the Property with the express or implied consent of the Tenant;

(b)   on or arising out of an alteration or addition to the Property or the installations in it carried out by the Tenant; or

(c)   which it is the responsibility of the Tenant to do.

10.3   The Landlord is not liable to the Tenant for breach of this clause unless the Landlord fails to carry out the work within a reasonable period after the Tenant has given the Landlord notice of the breach.]

11.   INSPECTIONS AND VIEWINGS

11.1   During the term

The Tenant must permit the Landlord, its employees or agents, and others authorised by the Landlord, on reasonable notice (except in an emergency), to enter the Property—

(a)   to examine its state and condition and how it is being used and to exercise any of the rights granted to the Landlord by this lease

(b)   to take inventories of the fixtures to be yielded up at the end of the term, and

(c)   to carry out repairs or alterations of or on adjoining premises or in connection with any pipes, drains, wires or services in or serving the Property.

11.2   At the end of the term

(a)   This subclause applies during the last 6 months of the term, or sooner if any money payable by the Tenant under this lease is more than a month overdue.

(b)   The Tenant will permit the Landlord to fix and keep notice boards of a reasonable size to conspicuous parts of the Property announcing that the Property is for sale or to be let.

(c)   The Tenant will permit the Landlord and its agents, and prospective buyers or lessees, to view the Property at reasonable times of the day.

11.3 **Making good**

The Landlord must make good all damage to the Property and tenant's fixtures caused by an entry.

12. **INSURANCE**

12.1 **Insurance by Landlord**

(a) The Landlord will insure the Property with a reputable insurer against—

- loss or damage by the insured risks in the sum which represents the full reinstatement cost, and

- professional fees and two years loss of rent.

(b) The Landlord's obligation under the preceding paragraph—

- does not apply if the insurance is invalidated by an act or omission of the Tenant or of the Tenant's employees, agents or visitors; and

- excludes all Property of the Tenant, Tenant's fixtures and fittings and plate glass, which are the Tenant's responsibility to insure.

(c) The Landlord need not maintain a separate policy of insurance for the Property but may insure by a block or general policy.

(d) The Landlord will lay out all money received in respect of its insurance (except sums in respect of loss of rent or professional fees) in rebuilding or reinstating that part of the Property destroyed or damaged.

(e) The Tenant may inspect the Landlord's insurance policy during normal office hours if the Tenant gives the Landlord at least seven days written notice.

12.2 **Insurance by Tenant**

(a) The Tenant will take out insurance with a reputable insurer against the following risks.

- breakage of the plate glass and windows at the Property

- liability or damage caused by plant or machinery in the Property

- damage by external signs such as A boards and hanging advertisements.

(b)   The Tenant will reinstate any asset for which the Tenant receives the money from its insurer.

(c)   The Tenant will produce his policy and the last premium receipt to the Landlord on request.

13.   SUSPENSION OF RENT IF PROPERTY DAMAGED OR DESTROYED BY INSURED RISKS

13.1   If the Property or an essential service or access to it is destroyed or damaged by any of the insured risks so as to make the Property unfit for occupation and use then, subject to the following paragraph, the rent (or a fair proportion of the rent according to the nature and extent of the damage sustained) will be suspended until whichever of the following events occurs first:

(a)   the Property, in the reasonable opinion of the Landlord, is again fit for occupation and use

(b)   expiry of the period covered by any loss-of-rent insurance

(c)   expiry of a notice of election given by either the Landlord or the Tenant under the next main clause (ending the lease if the Property is destroyed or damaged).

13.2   But this does not apply if—

(a)   the Property is destroyed or damaged by the act, default or negligence of the Tenant, or of the Tenant's employees, agents or visitors; or

(b)   the policy or policies of insurance effected by the Landlord have been invalidated, or payment of the policy money refused in whole or in part, in consequence of some act or default of the Tenant or the Tenant's employees, agents or visitors.

14.   ENDING LEASE IF THE PROPERTY IS DESTROYED OR DAMAGED

14.1   If the Property or an essential service or access is damaged by any of the insured risks so as to make the Property unfit for occupation and use and the relevant part cannot be reinstated without substantial rebuilding, the Landlord may elect to treat this lease as at an end and re-enter the Property on giving to the Tenant at least six months notice of that election.

14.2 If the Landlord has not begun to reinstate within the six months following the destruction or damage, the Tenant may elect to treat this lease as at an end and vacate the Property on giving to the Landlord not less than one month's notice of that election.

14.3 Any termination under this clause does not affect the rights of any party to recover in respect of any breach of any of the terms of this lease.

14.4 On service of a notice of election to treat the lease as at an end by either the Landlord or the Tenant all money received from the insurance effected by the Landlord under this lease belongs to the Landlord absolutely.

15. RE-ENTRY AND FORFEITURE

15.1 Each of the following is a forfeiting event within the meaning of this clause:

(a) the rent or any other sum payable by the Tenant under this lease is in arrears and unpaid for twenty one days after becoming payable (whether formally demanded or not)

(b) there is a breach by the Tenant of any of the tenant covenants in this lease

(c) a proposal is made in respect of the Tenant for a voluntary arrangement for a composition of debts or for a scheme of arrangement approved in accordance with the Insolvency Act 1986

(d) the Tenant becomes bankrupt

(e) an application is made to the court under the Insolvency Act 1986 in respect of the Tenant (being a company) for the appointment of an administrator

(f) the Tenant (being a company) enters into liquidation whether compulsory or voluntary (but not if the liquidation is for reconstruction of a solvent company) or has a receiver or manager of its business or undertaking, or has an administrative receiver (as defined in the Insolvency Act 1986) appointed, or

(g) the Tenant suffers any distress or execution to be levied on the Tenant's goods.

15.2   If and whenever a forfeiting event occurs, the Landlord may re-enter the Property at any time and this lease then comes to an end. Re-entry on part is to be treated as re-entry on the whole.

15.3   This right arises even if a previous right of re-entry has been waived.

15.4   Where the Tenant consists of more than one person, this right arises when a forfeiting event happens to one or more of them.

15.5   The ending of this lease under this clause does not affect the rights of any party in relation to any breach of the terms of this lease which occurred before this lease ended.

16.   **TENANT'S COMPENSATION ON QUITTING**

Subject to the provisions of section 38(2) of the Landlord and Tenant Act 1954, the Tenant is not entitled on vacating the Property to any compensation under section 37 of that Act.

17.   **LANDLORD'S RIGHT TO USE ADJOINING OR NEIGHBOURING LAND AND BUILDINGS**

17.1   The Landlord is entitled to deal as it thinks fit with any adjoining or neighbouring premises of the Landlord and to erect, or have erected, on that adjoining or neighbouring premises any buildings whatsoever, whether those buildings do or do not affect or diminish the light or air which may be enjoyed by the Property.

17.2   Nothing in this lease imposes any restriction on the use of any land or building not included in this lease. Nor does the Tenant have any standing in relation to the grant, enforcement, release or modification of land, assets or rights of any tenant or licensee of the Landlord relating to land or buildings not included in this lease.

18.   **LANDLORD'S NON-LIABILITY FOR ACCIDENTS ON THE PROPERTY**

18.1   The Landlord is not responsible to the Tenant or to anyone on the Property for—

(a)   accident or injury on the Property, including injury resulting in death; and

(b)   damage or loss to an asset on the Property.

18.2   This does not apply to the extent that the accident, injury, damage or loss occurs as a result of negligence on the part of the Landlord.

19.   NOTICES

19.1   In this lease, a notice includes a consent, request, demand and notification.

19.2   A notice under this lease must be given in writing.

19.3   The notice will be taken to be received—

(a)   on delivery, if served by hand

(b)   two working days after posting if sent by ordinary first-class post, unless it is returned undelivered

(c)   on the day of sending, if sent by recorded delivery post

(d)   on the day sent by fax, if sent before 3pm

(e)   on the next working day after being sent by fax if sent at 3pm or later.

19.4   Sending by email does not constitute good service under this lease.

19.5   The notice is taken to be delivered as follows:

(a)   to the Landlord, if left for or sent to its registered office

(b)   to an individual Tenant, if left for or sent to the Tenant at the address given in this lease or at the Property or at the Tenant's last known address or place of business in the United Kingdom

(c)   to a company Tenant, if left for or sent to the Tenant at the Tenant's registered office or the Property

(d)   to an individual guarantor, if left for or sent to the guarantor at the address given in this lease or at the guarantor's last known address or place of business in the United Kingdom

(e)   to a company guarantor, if left for or sent to the guarantor at the guarantor's registered office or at the guarantor's last known address or place of business in the United Kingdom.

20.   DISPUTE RESOLUTION

20.1   **Reference to arbitration**

Unless a particular clause provides otherwise, a difference between the parties arising from this lease is to be referred to a single arbitrator under the Arbitration Act 1996.

| 20.2 | **Appointment of arbitrator** |

In the absence of agreement, any party may apply at any time to the President of the Royal Institution of Chartered Surveyors for the appointment of an arbitrator.

| 20.3 | **Arbitrator unable to act** |

If an appointed arbitrator dies or is incapable of acting, any party may apply to the President of the Royal Institution of Chartered Surveyors for the appointment of a new arbitrator.

| 20.4 | **Reference to expert** |

The preceding paragraphs do not apply if the parties agree in writing that an expert would better settle a particular difference.

| 20.5 | **Referral back to arbitration** |

If the parties cannot agree on an expert within one month of that agreement, the paragraphs relating to arbitration reapply to the difference.

| 20.6 | **Expert's terms of employment** |

The expert's conditions of appointment must include—

(a) a requirement for the expert to consider any evidence or submissions made to him by the parties

(b) power for the expert to make an order for costs binding on all parties, and

(c) a provision that the expert's decision on questions of fact is binding on all parties.

21. NO WARRANTY ON USE

21.1 Nothing in this lease or in any consent granted under this lease implies that the Property may be used for any particular purpose under the Town and Country Planning Act 1990.

21.2 Nothing in this lease is to be interpreted as a warranty by the Landlord on the fitness, stability, soundness or suitability of the Property for use by the Tenant as permitted by this lease.

21.3 The Landlord does not warrant that the facilities at the Property are fit for the purpose for which the Tenant intends to use the Property or for any particular purpose. Usage of the Property is at the Tenant's risk. The Landlord is not responsible for any loss, injury, damage or expense which the Tenant may incur if the Property or its facilities prove defective or unfit for any particular purpose.

22.4 This does not apply where statute or this lease make express provision otherwise.

22. NO WAIVER OF COVENANTS

Each of the tenant covenants in this lease remains in full force even if the Landlord has—

22.1 temporarily waived or released another tenant covenant in this lease, or

22.2 varied, waived or released a similar covenant affecting premises belonging to the Landlord adjoining or nearby.

23. QUIET ENJOYMENT

The Landlord agrees with the Tenant that, provided the Tenant punctually pays the rent and observes the Tenant's obligations, the Tenant may peaceably use the Property without interruption by the Landlord or by anyone claiming under the Landlord.

24. CONTRACTS (RIGHTS OF THIRD PARTIES) ACT 1999

A person who is not a party to this lease has no right to enforce any of its terms.

25. RELEASE ON ASSIGNMENT OF REVERSION

On assignment of its reversion (however that happens) the Landlord is automatically released from the landlord covenants in this lease, regardless of the date a breach is alleged to have occurred.

26. COSTS OF THIS LEASE

The Tenant will pay the Landlord's reasonable legal costs in connection with the preparation and completion of this lease.

27. GUARANTOR'S OBLIGATIONS

27.1 **Liability periods**

A guarantor's liability under this clause lasts only while the particular guarantor is responsible, namely—

(a) in the case of the guarantor named as a party to this lease (or any person directly substituted for that guarantor) until that guarantor's principal is released

(b) in the case of a guarantor under an authorised guarantee agreement, as long as the relevant assignee is bound by the tenant covenants in this lease, and

(c)   in the case of a guarantor for a company on or before an assignment to that company, as long as the company is bound by the tenant covenants of this lease. —

27.2   **Main duties**

If the Tenant defaults on a tenant covenant in this lease (including default on payment of rent or other money) the guarantor must perform that covenant.

▶ [27.3 **New lease following disclaimer**

(a)   If the conditions set out in paragraph (b) apply, the guarantor must take a new lease of the Property from the Landlord on the basis set out in paragraph (c).

(b)   The conditions referred to in paragraph (a) are that—

- a trustee in bankruptcy or liquidator of the assignee has disclaimed the lease, and

- the Landlord has served a notice within 60 days of the Landlord becoming aware of the disclaimer.

(c)   The basis of the new lease is as follows:

- if this lease is one from which the provisions of sections 24 to 28 of the Landlord and Tenant Act 1954 are excluded, the new lease will also be one from which those provisions are excluded; and the guarantor will make a declaration or statutory declaration in accordance with schedule 2 of the Regulatory Reform (Business Tenancies) (England and Wales) Order 2003

- the commencement date is the date of the disclaimer

- the term is the residue of the contractual term of this lease at the date of the disclaimer

- the rent is the same as the rent then being paid under this lease, and

- the other provisions are the same as in this lease, except that the guarantor need not ensure that another person is joined as guarantor.

(d)   The guarantor must pay the costs of the new lease and execute a counterpart of it.]

27.4 Payments following disclaimer

(a) This subclause applies if this lease is disclaimed during the liability period and for any reason the Landlord does not require the guarantor to accept a new lease under this clause.

(b) The guarantor must pay the Landlord on demand the difference between the rent reserved by this lease and any money received by the Landlord for use and occupation of the Property.

(c) The period for which the guarantor must make this payment begins on the date of the disclaimer and ends on whichever is the earliest of—

- six months after the disclaimer

- the date on which the Property is relet

- the end of the term of this lease.

27.5 No release of guarantor

None of the following release or in any way affect the liability of the guarantor under this clause:

(a) grant by the Landlord of time or other indulgence to the Tenant

(b) neglect or abstention by the Landlord in enforcement of a tenant covenant

(c) refusal by the Landlord to accept rent at a time when it reasonably considered that to do so might amount to waiver of a right to forfeit

(d) variation of this lease

(e) surrender of part of the Property (in which case the liability of the guarantor extends only to the part of the Property not surrendered)

(f) any other happening by which, apart from this clause, the guarantor would have been released.

27.6 Tenant bound by authorised guarantee agreement

(a) This subclause applies if the Tenant is bound by an authorised guarantee agreement.

(b) If the Tenant defaults in his obligations under the authorised guarantee agreement, the guarantor will pay and make good to the Landlord on demand all losses, damages and costs arising from that failure.

(c)   None of the following release or in any way affect the liability of the guarantor under this subclause:

  •   grant by the Landlord of any time or other indulgence to the former tenant under the authorised guarantee agreement

  •   variation of the authorised guarantee agreement

  •   any other happening by which, apart from this clause, the guarantor would have been released.

27.7   **Replacement of guarantor**

(a)   In this subclause, references to a guarantor replacement event are (in the case of an individual) to death, bankruptcy, having a receiving order made or having a receiver appointed under the Mental Health Act 1983 and (in the case of a company) to passing a resolution to wind up, entering into liquidation or having a receiver appointed.

(b)   Where a guarantor replacement event occurs to any guarantor (including a guarantor under an authorised guarantee agreement) the Tenant must give notice of the event to the Landlord within 14 days of becoming aware of it.

(c)   If required by the Landlord, the Tenant must within 28 days obtain some other person acceptable to the Landlord to enter into a guarantee in the same form and to the same extent as the guarantee given by the other guarantor.

27.8   **Benefit passes with reversion**

The benefit of the guarantor's obligations attaches to the reversion on this lease without the need for any express assignment.

27.9   **Scope limited by Landlord and Tenant (Covenants) Act 1995**

A provision in this clause which extends beyond the limits permitted by the Landlord and Tenant (Covenants) Act 1995 is to be severed from the other provisions.

27.10   **Guarantor is principal debtor**

The guarantor is liable to the Landlord as principal debtor.

[▶28.   EXTENSION OF TERM

28.1   Holding over

This clause applies if after expiry of the term there is a period of holding over, extension or continuance, whether by agreement or operation of law.

28.2   Extension of the term

(a)   The provisions of this lease apply to that period.

(b)   The expression 'the term' will be interpreted as applying to that period.

(c)   References to the expiry of the term or the last year of the term will be to the end of that period however it comes to an end.

28.3   Periodic obligations

Obligations of a periodical nature will apply at the same intervals as those specified in this lease.

28.4   Rent review

The rent will only be reviewed after the expiry of the contractual term if this lease specifically provides for it. A provision by which a review period is defined as a period of years of the term will not be regarded as specific under this clause.]

[▶29.   TENANT'S RIGHT TO BREAK

29.1   Provided the precondition below is met, the Tenant may terminate this lease by [▶three] months notice to the Landlord given—

   (a)   after the expiry of the first [▶six] months of the term, and

   (b)   before the start of the last [▶six] months of the term.

29.2   Subject to the preceding subclause, the notice may expire at any time and not necessarily on a day for payment of rent.

29.3   The precondition is that on or before the expiry date of the notice, the Tenant must—

   (a)   have paid to the Landlord all rent and other sums due up to and including the expiry date of the notice

   (b)   have complied with the electricity inspection and gas servicing clauses of this lease, and

   (c)   give vacant possession of the Property.

29.4   As soon as practicable after termination, the Landlord will refund to the Tenant any rent or other payment made in advance for a period after termination.

[▶30.   SECURITY OF TENURE EXCLUDED

30.1   The Landlord and the Tenant agree that the provisions of sections 24 to 28 of the Landlord and Tenant Act 1954 (security of tenure) are excluded in relation to the tenancy created by this lease.

30.2   The Landlord has served the notice referred to in section 38A(3)(a) of the Act on the Tenant.

30.3   The Tenant has made a ▶ [statutory] declaration substantially in the form set out in schedule 2 to the Regulatory Reform (Business Tenancies) (England and Wales) Order 2003.]

[▶31.   WORKS BY TENANT

31.1   In this clause, "the works" means the operations specified in the timetable below.

31.2   The Tenant will carry out the works to the Property in accordance with the following timetable.

To be completed within ▶ [12 months] of the date of this lease

[*Insert works details*]

To be completed within ▶ [24 months] of the date of this lease

[*Insert works details*]

To be completed within ▶ [36 months] of the date of this lease

[*Insert works details*]

31.3   The Tenant will ensure that the works are done—

(a)   in accordance with planning legislation and building regulations, where these apply;

(b)   in compliance with the provisions of this lease;

(c)   to the satisfaction of the Landlord's surveyor; and

(d)   in a workmanlike way in accordance with best building practice.]

SCHEDULE 1

Rights granted with this letting

The Landlord grants the following non-exclusive rights.

1. **Services**

   The right of uninterrupted passage and running of gas, electricity, water, sewage, telephone, television and other services to and from the Property through the conducting media now or at any time during the term laid over the adjoining land of the Landlord.

   This right is not exclusive to the Tenant, but is shared with the Landlord and all other persons with similar rights.

▶[2. **Shelter, protection and support**

   The right of shelter, protection and support as now enjoyed by the Property from the adjoining land of the Landlord.]

▶[3. **Access**

   The right of access to and from the Property for the permitted use ▶[with or without vehicles] [on foot only] over the land shown ▶[coloured blue] on the attached plan.

▶[4. **Parking**

   The right to park ▶[one] car[s] or light van[s] in the parking space[s] designated in the Landlord's current parking scheme, with a vehicular right of access between the highway and the designated parking space[s].

   This right is subject to the Landlord's ability to replace the current parking Scheme from time to time by a revised scheme with the same number of parking spaces for the Tenant, which when notified to the Tenant supersedes all earlier schemes.]

SCHEDULE 2

Rights reserved from this letting

The Landlord retains the following rights for itself and its tenants, and all other persons nearby.

1. **Current services**

   Rights in respect of the Property corresponding to those granted to the Tenant by paragraph 1 of schedule 1.

2. **New services**

   The right to construct and maintain in, over or under the Property easements or services for the benefit of adjoining or nearby premises.

3. **Entry**

   The right at any time during the term, on reasonable notice to the Tenant (except in an emergency) to enter (or in an emergency during the Tenant's absence to break and enter) the Property in order—

   (a)   to inspect or carry out works in connection with any of the easements or services excepted or reserved by this lease

   (b)   to view the condition of the Property

   (c)   to carry out works upon any adjacent premises

   (d)   to carry out repairs or other works which should or may be carried out under the provisions of this lease by the Landlord or any other authorised person, or

   (e)   to carry out the Landlord's obligations under this lease.

4. **Works nearby**

   The right to rebuild or carry out other works to adjacent or nearby premises in whatever way the Landlord reasonably thinks fit, even if it interferes with light or air to the Property, and without liability to pay compensation.

▶[5.   **Shelter, protection and support**

   The right of shelter, protection and support from the Property as now enjoyed by the Landlord's adjoining land.]

▶[6.   **Repair of exterior**

The right to erect scaffolding for the purpose of repairing, maintaining or cleaning the exterior of the Property even if the scaffolding might temporarily interfere with access to or use of the Property.]

▶[7.   **Access for neighbour**

The right for the tenant and occupiers of [▶*address*] to pass and repass on foot over the part of the Property at ground floor level coloured [pink hatched red] on the attached plan.]

A person entering the Property to carry out works in exercise of the foregoing rights must cause as little disruption and damage as practicable and will make good all damage caused to the Property without delay.

SCHEDULE 3

Form of rent deposit agreement

DATE: **20▶**

PARTIES:

▶ [*insert full name and address of the Landlord, and in the case of a company, its company number and registered office address*] ("the Landlord") and

▶ [*insert full name and address of tenant, and in the case of a company, its company number and registered office address*] ("the Tenant").

1.   PAYMENT OF DEPOSIT

1.1   This deed is supplemental to a lease of ▶ [*insert address*] dated ▶ [the same as this deed] ▶ [*or insert other date*] made between the Landlord and ▶ [the Tenant] [▶ *insert original lessee, if not the Tenant*] ("the lease").

1.2   The Tenant has handed to the Landlord (and the Landlord acknowledges receipt) the sum of ▶ £ [*insert*] ("the deposit") to be held by the Landlord on the terms of this deed.

2.   APPLICATION OF DEPOSIT

2.1   The Landlord is entitled at any time to apply the whole or part of the deposit in payment of an amount owing to the Landlord as a result of the failure by the Tenant to pay—

2.1.1   the whole or part of the rents reserved by the lease

2.1.2   other money (including interest on rent arrears) payable under the lease

2.1.3   a cost or expense incurred by or payable to the Landlord in consequence of failure by the Tenant to observe the obligations on the part of the lessee under the lease.

2.2   Before applying any part of the deposit, the Landlord will first give the Tenant at least seven days written notice of its intention to do so. In that notice, the Landlord will specify the amount to be applied and the date on which the application is to be made.

3.   CHARGE OF DEPOSIT

3.1   The Tenant charges the deposit in favour of the Landlord as security for performance of the Tenant's obligations in the lease and in this deed.

3.2   The Tenant will pay the Landlord any fee to perfect the charge created.

4.   TOPPING UP DEPOSIT

4.1   The Tenant covenants with the Landlord during the term of the lease to maintain the deposit at the figure given in clause 1.

4.2   Whenever the Landlord applies any part of the deposit under clause 2, the Tenant will within seven days of the date specified in the Landlord's notice pay over to the Landlord a sum equal to the amount specified in that notice.

4.3   Any sum not paid within that seven-day period bears interest at 5% over the base lending rate from time to time of the Landlord's bank. Interest runs in the period beginning with the date specified in the Landlord's notice and ending with the date of payment.

5.   RETURN OF DEPOSIT

The Landlord will return the balance of the deposit (after first being applied in satisfaction of claims by the Landlord in accordance with clause 2) to the Tenant without interest on whichever of the following first occurs:

5.1   the lease comes to an end (however that is brought about)

5.2   the Tenant assigns the lease with the written consent of the Landlord in accordance with the provisions of the lease.

6.   SPECIAL POINTS

To avoid misunderstandings—

6.1   the Tenant is not entitled to interest on the deposit

6.2   tho liability of the Tenant is not limited to the deposit

6.3   the rights of the Landlord under this deed do not restrict the rights of the Landlord under the lease, and

6.4   the proviso for re-entry in the lease is exercisable on breach by the Tenant of an obligation in this deed as well as on the happening of the events mentioned in the lease.

7.   **THIRD PARTY RIGHTS EXCLUDED**

A person who is not a party to this deed has no right to enforce any of its terms.

Executed by all parties

SCHEDULE 4

Form of authorised guarantee agreement

DATE: 20►

PARTIES:

"the Guarantor" [*name*] of [*address, or in the case of company, registered office and company registration number*]

and

"the Landlord" [*name*] of [*address, or in the case of company, registered office and company registration number*]

1. **DEFINITIONS**

In this guarantee—

"the Assignee" means [► *insert full name*]

"the Lease" means the lease dated [► *insert*] and made between the Landlord and [► *insert*] and [► *insert*] for a term of [► *insert*] years [as varied by a deed dated [► *insert*] and made between [► *insert*]]

"the Property" means the premises demised by the Lease and known as [► *insert address*]

"the Liability Period" means the period during which the Assignee is bound by the Tenant covenants of the Lease; and

the expressions "authorised guarantee agreement" and "tenant covenants" have the same meaning as in the Landlord and Tenant (Covenants) Act 1995.

2. **BACKGROUND**

2.1 **Consent required**

In accordance with the terms of the Lease, the Landlord's consent to an assignment of it is required.

2.2 **Agreement to consent**

The Landlord has agreed to consent to the assignment of the Lease to the Assignee on condition that the Guarantor enters into this guarantee.

2.3 Effective time

This guarantee takes effect only when the Lease is assigned to the Assignee.

3. PERFORMANCE OF TENANT COVENANTS

3.1 If at any time during the Liability Period the Assignee defaults on a tenant covenant in the Lease (including default on payment of rent or other money) the Guarantor must perform that covenant.

3.2 This obligation applies even if—

(a) the Landlord has granted any time or other indulgence to the Assignee

(b) the Landlord has neglected or declined to enforce any tenant covenant

(c) the Landlord has refused to accept rent from the Assignee at a time when it reasonably considered that to do so might amount to waiver of the right to forfeit the Lease

(d) the provisions of the Lease have been varied

(e) the Assignee has surrendered part of the Property (in which case the liability of the Guarantor extends only to the part of the Property not surrendered) or

(f) anything else has occurred by which, apart from the clause, the Guarantor would have been released.

4. NEW LEASE FOLLOWING DISCLAIMER

4.1 If the conditions set out in clause 4.2 apply, the Guarantor must take a new lease of the Property from the Landlord on the basis set out in clause 4.3.

4.2 The conditions referred to in clause 4.1 are that—

(a) any trustee in bankruptcy or liquidator of the Assignee has disclaimed the Lease, and

(b) the Landlord has served notice on the Guarantor within 60 days of the Landlord becoming aware of the disclaimer.

4.3 The basis of the new lease is as follows:

(a) the commencement date is the date of the disclaimer

(b)   the term is the residue of the contractual term of the Lease at the date of the disclaimer

(c)   the rent is the same as the rent then being paid under the Lease, and

(d)   the other provisions are the same as in the Lease, except that the Guarantor need not ensure that any other person is joined as guarantor.

4.4   The Guarantor must pay the costs of the new lease and execute a counterpart of it.

5. PAYMENTS FOLLOWING DISCLAIMER

5.1   This clause applies if the Lease is disclaimed during the Liability Period and for any reason the Landlord does not require the Guarantor to accept a new lease under clause 4.

5.2   The Guarantor must pay the Landlord on demand the difference between the rent reserved by the Lease and any money received by the Landlord for use and occupation of the Property.

5.3   The period for which the Guarantor must make this payment begins on the date of the disclaimer and ends on whichever is the earliest of—

(a)   six months after the disclaimer

(b)   the date on which the Property is relet

(c)   the end of the contractual term of the Lease.

6. NOTIFICATION OF COMMITMENT END

The Landlord will notify the Guarantor in writing within 21 days of becoming aware of facts bringing the Liability Period to an end.

7. SCOPE LIMITED BY LANDLORD AND T ENANT (COVENANTS) ACT

Any provision in this agreement which extends beyond the limits permitted by the Landlord and Tenant (Covenants) Act 1995 is to be severed from the other provisions.

8. CONTRACTS (RIGHTS OF THIRD PARTIES) ACT 1999

The parties agree that a person who is not a party to this agreement has no right to enforce any terms of this agreement.

Executed by all parties

EXECUTED AS A DEED   )

by affixing the common seal of   )

)

in the presence of:)

Authorised officer

EXECUTED as a DEED by)

▶   LIMITED   )

acting by its officers:) Director

                                 Company secretary/Director

SIGNED as a DEED by   )

▶   )

in the presence of:)

Witness signature ....……………

Name of witness (printed) ....….………...

Address ....…………………….

....………….

....…………

Occupation ....…………………….

SIGNED as a DEED by   )

▶   )

in the presence of:)

Witness signature ....……………

Name of witness (printed) ....….………...

Address ....…………………….

....………….

....…………

Occupation ....…………………….

"LIBRARY OF CLAUSES" LEASE

This is a lease to build and manage student accommodation – though a change of use is contemplated (clause 5.1(b)). As it stands, it is too unusual for adoption wholesale. Because of uncertainties about income, planning consent and the gearing on rent, there are bound to be quirks that apply only to the particular circumstances of the grant in hand – for instance, the relationship between the premium and the initial rent. But the model does incorporate such a wide range of devices that it can be used as a depository of ideas that might be cut and pasted into other instruments. For example, it sets out the following.

- Base rents, followed by a rent as a percentage of gross income (clause 4.1 and 4.2 and schedule 4).

- The effect on rent of a change of use (clause 5.2).

- Extra steps to be taken before forfeiture (clause 11).

- Building obligations, including oversailing and the possibility of fresh planning permission (clause 20).

- Provision for a minimum rent (clause 4(1)(d) and schedule 3).

- Restrictions on alterations that might devalue adjoining property (clause 8.2).

- Rent review by reference to a price index (schedule 3).

Note that the prescribed clauses are part of the lease itself. Not only does this eliminate the awkward and unhelpful leaping about from clause to clause and from clause to schedule, it also minimises the possibility of mistakes. Trying to say the same thing more than once can lead to uncertainty, and sometimes to outright errors.

DATE: 2020

and

LEASE

of

LAND AT ▶

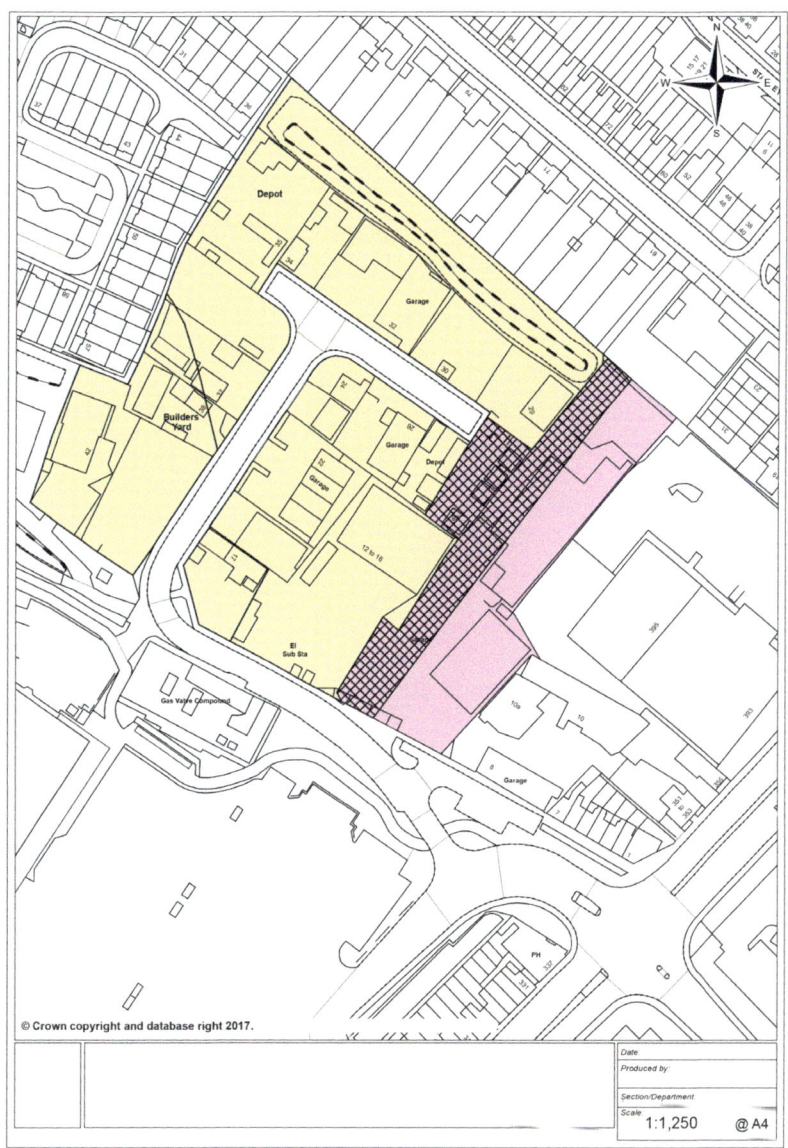

Depot

Garage

Builders
Yard

Garage

Garage

Depot

12 to 18

El
Sub Sta

Gas Valve Compound

Garage

PH

© Crown copyright and database right 2017.

| Date: |
| Produced by: |
| Section/Department: |
| Scale | 1:1,250 | @ A4 |

137

LR1. Date of lease	20▶
LR2. Title number(s)	**LR2.1 Landlord's title number(s)** ▶ **LR2.2 Other title numbers** NONE
LR3. Parties to this lease *Give full names, addresses and company's registered number, if any, of each of the parties. For Scottish companies use a SC prefix and for limited liability partnerships use an OC prefix. For foreign companies give territory in which incorporated.*	**Landlord** ▶ **Tenant** ▶ **Guarantor** ▶ NONE
LR4. Property	**In the case of a conflict between this clause and the remainder of this lease then, for the purposes of registration, this clause shall prevail.** The land at ▶ tinted pink and tinted pink hatched black on the attached plan
LR5. Prescribed statements etc	NONE
LR6. Term for which the Property is leased	The term is as follows: the period of 125 years beginning on the date of this lease
LR7. Premium	▶
LR8. Prohibitions or restrictions on disposing of this lease	This lease contains a provision that prohibits or restricts dispositions.
LR9. Rights of acquisition etc	**LR9.1 Tenant's contractual rights to renew this lease, to acquire the reversion or another lease of the Property, or to acquire an interest in other land** NONE **LR9.2 Tenant's covenant to (or offer to) surrender this lease** NONE **LR9.3 Landlord's contractual rights to acquire this lease** NONE

LR10. Restrictive covenants given in this lease by the Landlord in respect of land other than the Property	NONE
LR11. Easements	**LR11.1 Easements granted by this lease for the benefit of the Property** SCHEDULE 1 **LR11.2 Easements granted or reserved by this lease over the Property for the benefit of other property** SCHEDULE 2
LR12. Estate rentcharge burdening the Property	NONE
LR13. Application for standard form of restriction	NONE
LR14. Declaration of trust where there is more than one person comprising the Tenant *If the Tenant is one person, omit or delete all the alternative statements.* *If the Tenant is more than one person, complete this clause by omitting or deleting all inapplicable alternative statements.*	NOT APPLICABLE

1. INDEX OF DEFINITIONS AND DESCRIPTIONS

Clauses LR 1 to LR 14 contain some definitions, descriptions and explanations of words used in this lease. In addition, the expressions in this lease and set out in the left-hand column below are defined, used, described or explained in the places specified.

EXPRESSION	WHERE DEFINED
"the £150,000 period"	Clause 4(1)(c)
accounting year	Clause 4.1(e)
the minimum rent	Schedule 3
first occupied	Clause 4(1)(b)
first rent payment day	Clause 4(3)(b)
"gross income"	Clause 4.2 and Schedule 4
"the Property"	Clause LR 4
rent payment days	Clause 4(3)(a)
"tenant covenants"	The Landlord and Tenant (Covenants) Act 1995
"the term"	Clause LR 6
"the alterations zone"	Clause 8.2(a)
"the works"	Clause 20

2. GENERAL INTERPRETATION

2.1 Gender and number

Words of one gender include any other gender, and the singular includes the plural and vice versa.

2.2 Joint and several benefit and liability

Where a party consists of more than one person, the rights and obligations of that party under this lease are rights and obligations of those persons separately, all together or in any combination.

2.3 Corporations

A person includes a company or other body corporate.

2.4 Obligations

A Tenant's obligation not to do anything includes an obligation not to allow that thing to be done by another person.

2.5 **Amendment or repeal of statutes**

(a) Reference to a repealed Act of Parliament is a reference to the Act which, with or without modification, replaces or corresponds to the repealed Act.

(b) Reference to an Act of Parliament which has been amended is a reference to that Act as amended.

(c) This subclause does not apply to the Town and Country Planning (Use Classes) Order 1987.

3. LETTING

In return for the premium (receipt of which the Landlord acknowledges) and with full title guarantee, the Landlord lets the Property to the Tenant for the term with the rights specified in schedule 1, but retaining the rights set out in schedule 2.

4. RENT AND OTHER PAYMENTS BY TENANT

4.1 **Amount of rent**

(a) The amount of rent is as follows.

(b) Until any residential accommodation on the Property is first occupied by a student under a lease or licence, or for three years after the grant of this lease (whichever is the shorter) £▶ a year.

(c) From the end of the period in (b) until the first rent payment day following the end of the next five years ("the £150,000 period") £150,000 a year.

(d) For every accounting year after the £150,000 period, whichever is the higher of—

(i) 6.53% of the gross income received by the Tenant in that year, or another percentage found under clause 5.2 (change of use);

(ii) the minimum rent found in accordance with schedule 3; or

(e) For the purposes of this lease, an accounting year is every annual cycle beginning at the end of the £150,000 period.

(f) The Tenant will notify the Landlord immediately any unit is first occupied, but this exercise need only be carried out once.

(g) Time is of the essence of the three-year period in (b) above.

4.2 Definition of "gross income"

(a) "Gross income" is the gross income for one accounting year received by the Tenant from the buildings on the Property.

(b) Schedule 4 contains further provisions about the gross income and the rent.

4.3 Payment of rent

(a) Subject to clause 5, the Tenant promises to pay the rent to the Landlord without deduction or set-off by equal instalments in advance on the usual quarter days namely 25 March, 24 June, 29 September and 25 December each year.

(b) The first rent payment is due on the date of this lease for the period starting with the beginning of the term and ending on the day before the rent payment day following the date of this lease.

(d) If payment starts or ends partway through a payment period, the rent will be apportioned on a daily basis.

(e) The rent is exclusive of outgoings.

4.4 After the £150,000 period: payments on account

On each rent payment day after the end of the £150,000 period the Tenant will pay the Landlord (in advance and on account of the total rent payable for that year) one quarter of the rent payable for the preceding year.

4.4 Balancing payment

Within 28 days of the end of each accounting year the Tenant will—

(a) deliver the audit certificate to the Landlord in accordance with schedule 4 showing the gross income received from the Property; and

(b) either pay the balance of the rent for that year found in accordance with clause 4.1(d), taking account of the payments already made; or receive a refund form the Landlord of any overpayment.

4.5 Outgoings

(a) The Tenant must pay all outgoings that are now or may at any time during the term be charged, assessed or imposed upon the Property or upon the owner or occupier of it, excluding any payable by the Landlord on rent received or on a dealing with this lease or arising from the Landlord's ownership of the freehold of the Property. Subject to the next paragraph, the Tenant must pay the appropriate authority direct.

(b)   Where outgoings are assessed by reference to the Property jointly with other premises, the Tenant must pay to the Landlord the proportion reasonably Attributed to the Property by the Landlord.

(c)   Subject to receipt of a proper VAT invoice, the Tenant must pay all value added tax that may from time to time be charged on the rent or other sums payable by the Tenant under this lease.

4.6 Interest on late payment of sums due to the Landlord

If either party fails to pay any sum due under this lease within14 days of the due date, it must pay the other interest on the amount owing (at the rate of 3% above the base rate of Barclays Bank for the time being) from the date when it was due to the date on which it is actually paid.

4.7 Costs of service of notices

The Tenant must pay on demand all expenses (including solicitors' costs and surveyors' fees) reasonably and properly incurred by the Landlord which arise from, or are incidental to—

(a)   the preparation and service of a notice under section 146 of the Law of Property Act 1925

(b)   the taking of proceedings under sections 146 and 147 of that Act whatever the outcome of those proceedings, and

(c)   the preparation and service of notices and schedules relating to repair of the Property, whether served before or within 6 months of the ending of this lease.

4.8 Shared facilities

The Tenant agrees to contribute a reasonable and proper proportion of the expense of repairing, maintaining and cleaning all party walls and all sewers, drains, conduits and service media used by the occupier of the Property in common with occupiers of premises adjoining or nearby.

4.7   **Payments treated as rent**

All payments due from the Tenant to the Landlord under this lease are to be treated as rent.

5.   **USE OF THE PROPERTY**

5.1   **Use**

The Tenant may use the Property—

(a)   during the first 30 years of the term as ▶accommodation for students in higher or further education, and (in vacation periods) for ancillary uses as allowed by the planning permission under which the buildings on the Property are being operated; and

(b)   during the remainder of the term for any other use which the Landlord from time to time approves. The Landlord is entitled to refuse approval without qualification to a use within class C3 of the Town and Country Planning (Use Classes) Order 1987, but otherwise the Landlord may not unreasonably withhold or delay approval. That approval is not to be subject to the payment of a fine or premium or to an increase in rent or to any other financial gain to the Landlord.

5.2   **Change of use**

(a)   This subclause applies to a proposed change of use under clause 5.1(b).

(b)   Where the parties reasonably consider that clause 4.2 (definition of gross income) cannot practically be applied to the proposed use, they will seek to agree a change in the calculation of rent so that the rent payable under this lease represents fair market practice at the date the Tenant begins the proposed use.

(c)   Until the proposed permitted use begins, the provisions of this lease continue to apply.

(d)   Differences under this subclause are to be dealt with under clause 16 (dispute resolution).

5.3   **Dangerous materials**

The Tenant must not bring on to or store at the Property any article, substance or liquid of a specially combustible, inflammable radioactive or dangerous nature.

5.4 **Nuisance notice**

(a) If the Landlord gives notice to the Tenant requiring the stopping of an actionable nuisance caused by vibration, noise or offensive smell, or by undue emissions of smoke, gas, fumes, vapour or dust, the Tenant must stop the nuisance immediately.

(b) Exercise of the right in this subclause is subject to the requirements—

(i) of the Tenant to develop and redevelop the Property; and

(ii) for the Landlord to act reasonably.

5.5 **Obstruction of highway**

Except where consent has been obtained from the highway authority, the Tenant must not place any goods, machine, caseboard, or other material near the Property or in the adjacent highway, or obstruct the highway in any way.

5.6 **Management of easements and encroachment**

(a) The Tenant may grant easements and wayleaves in the normal course of the works and in its management of the Property throughout the term. At the reasonable request from and at the cost of the Tenant, the Landlord will enter into any deed of easement or wayleave agreement reasonably required by the Tenant in a form approved by the Landlord. That approval may not be withheld or delayed unreasonably.

(b) Subject to the preceding paragraph the Tenant must take all reasonable steps to prevent a trespass upon the Property or the acquisition of any new right to light, right of way, right of drainage or other easement over, on or under the Property.

(c) The Tenant must give notice to the Landlord of any threatened trespass or attempt to acquire an easement or right of the kind referred to in paragraph (b) as soon as the Tenant becomes aware of it.

(d) If reasonably requested by the Landlord, the Tenant must stop the trespass, acquisition of an easement or right of that kind.

(d) The Tenant must allow the Landlord (on reasonable notice and at reasonable times except in an emergency) to enter any part of the Property not built on to do anything reasonably necessary to prevent an encroachment or acquisition of an easement or right.

5.7   **Discharge into pipes and drains**

(a)   The Tenant must not discharge any oil, grease, acid or other noxious, toxic or corrosive substance into any pipe or drain serving the Property—

  (i)   which may cause an obstruction in, or damage to, any such pipe or drain; or

  (ii)   to which any water or sewerage company or other competent authority may object.

(b)   If a discharge occurs, the Tenant must as soon as reasonably practicable—

  (i)   make good any obstruction or damage to the reasonable satisfaction of the Landlord and the water or sewerage company or other competent authority; and

  (ii)   comply with the reasonable requirements of the Landlord and the water or sewerage company or other competent authority to remedy the discharge or passage or to prevent its recurrence.

5.8   **Damage or injury arising from the Tenant's use of the Property**

The Tenant must indemnify the Landlord against all losses, claims and expense arising directly or indirectly from—

(a)   the Tenant's use and occupation of the Property

(b)   an act, omission, negligence or default of the Tenant (or of the employees, agents, licensees or visitors of the Tenant), or

(c)   a breach by the Tenant of any of the terms of this lease.

5.9   **Compliance with law and statutory directions**

(a)   The Tenant must comply with all statutes, regulations, orders, statutory instruments and byelaws whether made before or after the date of this lease and with all lawful directions and requirements of any local or public authority in respect of the Property or the Tenant's occupation or use of the Property.

(b)   The Tenant must carry out all works required in respect of the Property by or under statutes, regulations, orders, statutory instruments and byelaws whether made before or after the date of this lease.

5.10   **Notices affecting the Property**

If the Tenant receives a communication from a competent authority affecting or likely to affect the Property, the Tenant must—

(a)   as soon as reasonably practicable send details to the Landlord

(b)   without delay and if appropriate, take all reasonable steps to comply with the communication at the Tenant's expense, and

(c)   join with the Landlord in making any representation to the communicating authority reasonably required by the Landlord. If the incidence or the amount of the cost cannot be agreed, the matter is to be decided in accordance with the dispute resolution clause in this lease.

6.   PLANNING REQUIREMENTS

6.1   **Breach of planning control**

The Tenant must not commit a breach of planning control.

6.2   **Charge on breach of planning control**

The Tenant must pay and satisfy any charge that may be imposed on breach by the Tenant of planning control or otherwise under the Town and Country Planning Act 1990.

7.   DEALINGS

7.1   **General prohibition**

(a)   Except as provided in this clause, the Tenant may not deal with this lease, or part with or share possession or occupation of the Property or any part of it.

(b)   To "deal with" includes to assign, charge or underlet in whole or in part, and to hold on trust for another; and "dealing" is to be interproted accordingly

(c)   The following do not constitute breaches of this clause:

i)   provided no landlord and tenant relationship is established, sharing the whole or part of the Property with a company that is a member of the same group as the Tenant within section 42 of the Landlord and Tenant Act 1954;

(ii)   leasing or licensing any individual unit at the Property for a period of up to one year;

(iii)   leasing or licensing any part of the Property to a person who provides a service to the occupiers of the residential accommodation at the Property (for example a doctors' surgery, gym, laundry, concession kiosk or canteen) for a period of up to five years (which may be renewed); and

(iv)   entry for the benefit of the Property into a wayleave agreement, or a telecommunications or substation lease with a services or utilities provider.

7.2   Assignment of whole

(a)   General rule

Until the last seven year of the term, the Tenant may assign the Property as a whole.

(b)   Last seven years of the term

In the last seven years of the term, the Tenant may assign the Property as a whole if the Tenant first—

(i)   obtains the consent of the Landlord in the form of a licence to assign under seal (and that licence is not to be unreasonably withheld or delayed)

(ii)   satisfies the circumstances referred to in (c) below, and

(iii)   complies with the condition set out in (d) below.

The circumstances and condition are prescribed for the purposes of the Landlord and Tenant Act 1927 section 19(1A).

(c)   Circumstances

The circumstances referred to are that all sums payable by the Tenant under this lease must be paid up to the date of the assignment.

(d)   Condition

The condition referred to is that on completion of the licence to assign, the outgoing tenant or the assignee must pay the Landlord's reasonable legal and surveyors' costs and fees incurred.

7.3 **Charge of whole**

(a) Until the last seven years of the term the Tenant may mortgage, hold on trust or charge the whole of the Property.

(b) During the last seven years of the term, the Tenant is not to mortgage hold on trust or charge the whole of the Property without the Landlord's consent, and that consent may not be withheld or delayed unreasonably.

7.4 **Underletting**

(a) The Tenant may underlet the accommodation blocks at the Property separately, all together or in any combination for terms less than 25 years.

(b) With the consent of the Landlord (and that consent may not be withheld or delayed unreasonably) the Tenant may underlet the accommodation blocks at the Property separately, all together or in any combination for terms of 25 years or more.

(c) The Tenant may underlet the Property as a whole for a term of 21 years or more (and for as long as the undertenant remains in the same group as the Tenant within the meaning of section 42 of the Landlord and Tenant Act 1954) on terms which are substantially the same as those contained in this lease except for the amount of rent.

(d) All underlettings under this subclause must exclude sections 24 to 28 of the Landlord and Tenant Act 1954 from the subtenancy in accordance with section 38A of that Act.

7.5 **Registration of dealings**

(a) Within one month of a dealing with the Property, the Tenant must—

(i) give notice of it to the Landlord and pay the Landlord's reasonable charges for registration of each dealing, and

(ii) send the Landlord a copy of the document by which the dealing was carried out.

(b) Leases or licences of individual units are not registrable with the Landlord.

8. MAINTENANCE, REPAIR AND ALTERATION

8.1 Maintaining the Property

The Tenant must keep the external fabric of the buildings on the Property in repair and good condition, must keep the external areas neat and tidy, and must maintain boundary structures on all sides of the Property.

8.2 Alterations and additions to the Property

(a) The Tenant must not make a structural alteration or addition to the parts of the buildings from time to time lying within that section of the Property hatched black on the attached plan ("the alterations zone") without first—

    (i) obtaining the consent of the Landlord (and that consent is not to be unreasonably withheld or delayed);

    (ii) obtaining any planning permission or building consent which may be required; and

    (iii) paying the Landlord's reasonable legal and surveyors' costs and fees.

(b) The Tenant must comply with all conditions of those permissions and consents.

(c) It will always be reasonable for the Landlord to withhold its consent under paragraph (a) (i) if the grant of planning permission would have materially adverse consequences on the value either of the Property or of the Landlord's nearby land shown yellow on the attached plan.

(d) Paragraph (a) does not apply to—

    (i) the implementation of planning permission ▶ [*insert number*] (and any permitted variation of it);

    (ii) the implementation of any substituted planning permission under clause 20.2;

    (iii) the erection or removal of internal demountable partitioning;

    (iv) compliance with statute or regulations; or

    (v) an external alteration or external addition to the non-built upon areas of the alterations zone where the nature and extent of the alteration does not create a new structure over 3 metres high.

9. INSPECTIONS AND VIEWINGS

9.1 During the term

The Tenant must permit the Landlord, its employees or agents, and others authorised by the Landlord, on reasonable notice (except in an emergency), to enter the Property at reasonable times—

(a)   to examine its state and condition and how it is being used and to exercise any of the rights granted to the Landlord by this lease

(b)   to carry out repairs or alterations of or on adjoining premises or in connection with any pipes, drains, wires or services in or serving the Property; but this right may only be exercised on a part of the Property not built on.

9.2 At the end of the term

(a)   This subclause applies during the last 6 months of the term.

(b)   The Tenant will permit the Landlord to fix and keep notice boards of a reasonable size to conspicuous parts of the Property announcing that the Property is for sale or to be let.

(c)   The Tenant will permit the Landlord and its agents, and prospective buyers or lessees, to view the Property at reasonable times of the day and on reasonable notice.

9.3 Making good

To the Tenant's reasonable satisfaction and as soon as reasonably practicable, the Landlord must make good all damage to the Property and tenant's fixtures caused by an entry.

10. INSURANCE

10.1   The Tenant will insure the Property with a reputable insurer against loss or damage by fire and other risks in the sum which represents the full reinstatement cost.

10.2   The Tenant need not maintain a separate policy of insurance for the Property but may insure by a block or general policy.

10.3   The Tenant will lay out all money received in respect of its insurance (except sums in respect of loss of rent or professional fees) in rebuilding or reinstating that part of the Property destroyed or damaged.

10.4   The Tenant will supply evidence of its insurance to the Landlord on reasonable request.

11. RE-ENTRY AND FORFEITURE

11.1 What is a forfeiting event

Each of the following is a forfeiting event within the meaning of this clause:

(a)   the rent or any other sum payable by the Tenant under this lease is in arrears and unpaid for twenty-eight days after becoming payable (whether formally demanded or not)

(b)   there is a material breach by the Tenant of any of the tenant covenants in this lease.

11.2 Notice to Tenant

Before beginning proceedings for forfeiture of this lease, the Landlord must—

(a)   notify the breach complained of to the Tenant; and

(b)   allow the Tenant a reasonable time to remedy it.

11.3 Notice to mortgagee

If the Tenant fails to comply with that notification, the Landlord must—

(a)   notify the breach to any mortgagee of which the Landlord has notice; and

(b)   allow the mortgagee a reasonable time to remedy it.

11.4 Forfeiture action

Subject to the preceding subclauses, if and whenever a forfeiting event occurs, the Landlord may re-enter the Property at any time and this lease then comes to an end. Re-entry on part is to be treated as re-entry on the whole.

11.5 Earlier waiver

This right in the preceding subclause arises even if a previous right of re-entry has been waived.

11.6 Where Tenant is more than one person

Where the Tenant consists of more than one person, this right arises when a forfeiting event happens to one or more of them.

11.7 **Effect of forfeiture**

The ending of this lease under this clause does not affect the rights of any party in relation to any breach of the terms of this lease which occurred before this lease ended.

12. **TENANT'S COMPENSATION ON QUITTING**

Subject to the provisions of section 38(2) of the Landlord and Tenant Act 1954, the Tenant is not entitled on vacating the Property to any compensation under section 37 of that Act.

13. **LANDLORD'S NON-LIABILITY FOR ACCIDENTS ON THE PROPERTY**

13.1 The Landlord is not responsible to the Tenant or to anyone on the Property for—

(a) accident or injury on the Property, including injury resulting in death; and

(b) damage or loss to an asset on the Property.

13.2 This does not apply to the extent that the accident, injury, damage or loss occurs as a result of negligence on the part of the Landlord.

14. **NOTICES**

14.1 **What is a notice**

In this lease, a notice includes a consent, request, demand, approval and notification.

14.2 **Writing required**

A notice under this lease must be in writing.

14.3 **Time**

The notice will be taken to be received—

(a) on delivery, if served by hand

(b) two working days after posting if sent by ordinary first-class post, unless it is returned undelivered

(c) on the day of sending, if sent by recorded delivery post

(d) on the day sent by fax, if sent before 3pm

(e) on the next working day after being sent by fax if sent at 3pm or later.

14.4   **Email**

Sending by email does not constitute good service under this lease.

14.5   **Place**

The notice is taken to be delivered as follows:

(a)   to the Landlord, if left for or sent to ▶

(b)   to an individual Tenant, if left for or sent to the Tenant at the address given in this lease or at the Property or at the Tenant's last known address or place of business in the United Kingdom

(c)   to a company Tenant, if left for or sent to the Tenant at the Tenant's registered office or the Property

(d)   to an individual guarantor, if left for or sent to the guarantor at the address given in this lease or at the guarantor's last known address or place of business in the United Kingdom

(e)   to a company guarantor, if left for or sent to the guarantor at the guarantor's registered office or at the guarantor's last known address or place of business in the United Kingdom.

15.   DISPUTE RESOLUTION

15.1   **Reference to arbitration**

Unless a particular clause provides otherwise, a difference between the parties arising from this lease is to be referred to a single arbitrator under the Arbitration Act 1996.

15.2   **Appointment of arbitrator**

In the absence of agreement, any party may apply at any time to the President of the Royal Institution of Chartered Surveyors for the appointment of an arbitrator.

15.3   **Arbitrator unable to act**

If an appointed arbitrator dies or is incapable of acting, any party may apply to the President of the Royal Institution of Chartered Surveyors for the appointment of a new arbitrator.

15.4   **Reference to expert**

The preceding paragraphs do not apply if the parties agree in writing that an expert would better settle a particular difference.

15.5   **Referral back to arbitration**

If the parties cannot agree on an expert within one month of that agreement, the paragraphs relating to arbitration reapply to the difference.

15.6   **Expert's terms of employment**

The expert's conditions of appointment must include—

(a)   a requirement for the expert to consider any evidence or submissions made to him by the parties

(b)   power for the expert to make an order for costs binding on all parties, and

(c)   a provision that the expert's decision on questions of fact is binding on all parties.

16.   NO WARRANTY ON USE

16.1   Nothing in this lease or in any consent granted under this lease implies that the Property may be used for any particular purpose under the Town and Country Planning Act 1990.

16.2   Nothing in this lease is to be interpreted as a warranty by the Landlord on the fitness, stability, soundness or suitability of the Property for use by the Tenant as permitted by this lease.

16.3   The Landlord does not warrant that the facilities at the Property are fit for the purpose for which the Tenant intends to use the Property or for any particular purpose. Usage of the Property is at the Tenant's risk. The Landlord is not responsible for any loss, injury, damage or expense which the Tenant may incur if the Property or its facilities prove defective or unfit for any particular purpose.

16.4   This does not apply where statute or this lease make express provision otherwise.

17. **NO WAIVER OF COVENANTS**

Each of the tenant covenants in this lease remains in full force even if the Landlord has—

17.1   temporarily waived or released another tenant covenant in this lease, or

17.2   varied, waived or released a similar covenant affecting premises belonging to the Landlord adjoining or nearby.

18. **QUIET ENJOYMENT**

The Landlord agrees with the Tenant that the Tenant may peaceably use the Property without interruption by the Landlord or by anyone claiming under the Landlord.

19. **RELEASE ON ASSIGNMENT OF REVERSION**

On assignment of its reversion (however that happens) the Landlord is automatically released from the landlord covenants in this lease, regardless of the date a breach is alleged to have occurred.

20. **WORKS BY TENANT**

20.1   **Meaning of "the works"**

(a)   in this lease, "the works" means the operations—

(i)   under planning permission ▶ [*insert number*] or under any substituted planning permission within the subclause that follows

(ii)   specified in the associated agreement under section 106 of the Town and Country Planning Act 1990, and

(iii)   on plans and specifications submitted to and agreed by the Landlord.

(b)   The Tenant will submit to the Landlord plans and specifications for the works as soon as practicable after they have been drawn up. The Landlord may act as a landowner (as opposed to acting as a planning authority) but may not withhold its agreement unreasonably.

20.2   **Substituted planning permission**

(a)   The Tenant may submit a fresh planning application for a revised student accommodation scheme in substitution for planning permission ▶ [*insert number*].

(b)   Before submitting that fresh planning application, the Tenant must liaise with the Landlord on its proposals with a view to the substituted planning application—

    (i)   being for a student accommodation scheme of a similar design, scale and massing,

    (ii)   being more aligned with the Tenant's business model for student accommodation

    (iii)   maximizing the income generated by the development; and

    (iv)   allowing for a variation of the gross external area of the development of up to 15% of the gross external area of the scheme under planning permission ▶ [*insert number*].

    (v)   having proportionately as many units of accommodation and other rentable spaces on the Property as in planning application ▶ [*insert number*].

(c)   The Tenant will supply the Landlord with copies of all plans and specifications in connection with any substituted application.

20.3   **Start and finish promptly**

The Tenant will ensure that the works are begun and completed as soon as possible and in any event by the end of the £150,000 period.

20.4   **Oversailing**

To the extent that the Landlord is able to do so (and at the Tenant's cost) the Landlord will grant to the Tenant on reasonable request a free oversailing licence in the form the Landlord reasonably requires, taking into account (amongst other things) the type of development being undertaken by the Tenant and the use of the Landlord's adjoining land.

20.5   **General standards**

The Tenant will ensure that the works are carried out—

(a)   in accordance with planning legislation and building regulations;

(b)   in compliance with the provisions of this lease;

(c)   to the reasonable satisfaction of the Landlord's surveyor; and

(d)   in a workmanlike way and in accordance with good building practice.

SCHEDULE 1

Right granted with this letting

The Landlord grants the following rights.

1.   **Services**

(a)   The rights of uninterrupted passage and running of gas, electricity, water, sewage, telephone, television and other services to and from the Property through the conducting media now laid over the adjoining land of the Landlord; together with the right to connect into those conducting media so long as the connection is made within the Property.

(b)   Where any service used by the Tenant is to be stopped up or relocated by the Landlord, the Landlord is to provide an alternative service. The Landlord will grant to the Tenant upon reasonable request a right to connect into that alternative service, and to use it. This right to connect is limited to connecting within the Property where the Landlord has ensured that the relocated service extends to the boundary between the Property and the Landlord's adjoining land.

2.   **Access to repair services**

(a)   The right on not less than 72 hours notice (except in an emergency) to enter those parts of the Landlord's adjoining land (but not any buildings) as may be reasonably required to clean, maintain, inspect and repair the conducting media used under paragraph 1.

(b)   This right is subject to the following qualifications, requirements and needs.

        (i)   The works cannot be carried out reasonably and economically from the Property.

        (ii)   The Tenant must act reasonably.

        (iii)   The Tenant must ensure that the person entering the Landlord's adjoining land causes as little disruption and damage as practicable and makes good all damage to the Landlord's adjoining land without delay and to the reasonable satisfaction of the Landlord.

(iv)   The need for the Landlord to develop and redevelop its adjoining land.

3.   Support and protection

Rights of support and protection from the Landlord's adjoining land.

4.   Light and air

The right to develop and use the Property in whatever way the Tenant may wish, even though the development or use interferes with the access of light and air to the Landlord's adjoining land.

These rights are not exclusive to the Tenant, but are shared with the Landlord and all other persons with similar rights.

SCHEDULE 2

Rights reserved from this letting

The Landlord retains rights in respect of the Property corresponding to those granted to the Tenant by schedule 1.

SCHEDULE 3

Minimum rent under clause 4(1)(d)

1. **Review period**

   The minimum rent is to be reviewed every 15 years. The first review is to take   place on the first day of the month following 15 years after the start of the £150,000 period. Subsequent reviews follow at 15-year intervals.

2. **Review process**

   At each review, the minimum rent is to be fixed at the higher of—

   (a)   the rent immediately before that review; or

   (b)   the figure found in accordance with following formula:

   $$A \times \frac{C}{B} \quad \text{where—}$$

   A is the rent immediately before that review;

   B is the figure in CPI (see below) for the month two months before the start of the review period or (in the case of the first review) the figure in CPI for the month two months before the start of the £150,000 period; and

   C is the figure in CPI for the month two months before the relevant review date.

3. **Cap on annual increase**

   (a)   This paragraph applies if in any year of a 15-year review period the increase in the CPI exceeds 4%. A year starts on a review date or (in the case of the first review period) on the first day of the month following the end of the £150,000 period.

   (b)   In that event, the calculation under paragraph 2 is to be made year on year over the review period using the CPI increase for each year, but capping the increase at 4% where the annual CPI increase exceeds this. The new minimum rent will then be the preceding minimum rent plus the cumulative total of the annual increases for each year of the review period.

4.   **Meaning of "CPI"**

In this schedule, "CPI" means the general index of consumer prices (for all items) published by the Statistics Board or, if that index is not published for a relevant month, any substituted index or index figures published by the Board.

5.   **Notice of reviewed rent**

The Landlord must notify the Tenant as soon as possible after a new minimum rent has been found.

6.   **Memorandum**

The parties will endorse on or securely attach to this lease and its counterpart a memorandum of each reviewed minimum rent, signed by the Landlord and the Tenant. Each party is to bear its own cost of this exercise.

7.   **Effect of delay in notifying revised minimum rent**

(a)   Between (i) any review date and (ii) finding and notifying the new minimum rent, rent will continue to be payable at the rate immediately before that review date.

(b)   Following notification of the revised minimum rent, and within 10 working days of a demand from the Landlord, the Tenant will pay to the Landlord as a lump sum any difference between the amount the Tenant has actually paid and the amount that would have been payable had the revised minimum rent been notified before the review date.

8.   **Time not of the essence**

Time is not of the essence of any step in this schedule.

SCHEDULE 4

Gross income

1.   **What is included**

(a)   There is to be included in the calculation of gross income—

- the rents, licence fees or other financial consideration from the use and occupation of any part of the Property which the Tenant actually receives, including the entirety of "all-inclusive" rents paid under student tenancy agreements

- any shortfall of rent or fee resulting from ascertainment of an increase after the increase was due, and any associated interest payable

- any insurance proceeds the Tenant is entitled to receive for loss of income from a unit damaged or destroyed.

(b)   Where the Tenant is not the person immediately entitled to the income, references to the Tenant are to that other person, with the intention that the Landlord has a share in the rent or licence fee actually paid by the end user of the Property or parts of it (which at the date of this lease will primarily be the students occupying the student accommodation to be constructed by the Tenant).

(c)   Where a financial consideration relates to an area partially within and partially outside the Property, the income is to be apportioned.

(d)   In calculating the gross income, there is to be no double counting of payments.

2.   **What is not included**

The following are not to be included in the calculation:

- VAT actually received by the Tenant

- deductions resulting directly or indirectly from a default by the Tenant in performing its obligations as licensor or under statute

- interest payable by occupiers of units for overdue payment of fees or other   money due to the Tenant from the occupier

- money held under a trust, in escrow, as stakeholder or in a similar arrangement

- money refundable to an occupier, while it remains refundable

- reimbursement of the Tenant where the Tenant has paid a third party direct, after the occupier has failed to

- payments made by an occupier to a third party (for example payments for television, mobile telephone, broadband, internet and insurance services)

- payments made by an occupier to a third party service provider (for example a doctors' surgery, gym, concession kiosk or canteen)

- a premium or similar payment on the grant of a bona fide long lease

- any payment not generally reserved as gross income but stated in the letting document to be recoverable as rent or treated or regarded as rent in the enforcement of tenant covenants.

3.   **Assumptions**

In calculating the gross income it is to be assumed that a damaged or destroyed unit has been fully restored.

4.   **Keeping records**

(a)   Throughout the term the Tenant must keep accurate and up-to-date accounting records of all rents, fees and other monetary receipts paid to payable by occupiers of units.

(b)   On at least fifteen working days' notice, the Tenant must make those records available for inspection by the Landlord.

5.   **Audit of accounts**

(a)   The Tenant must have all accounting records required under this schedule and in respect of all sums payable as rent under this lease audited by an independent chartered or certified accountant within three months of the end of each accounting year.

(b)   The auditor must act in accordance with professional practice and accounting standards applicable from time to time.

(c)   The Tenant must produce to the Landlord—

- an audit certificate from the auditor addressed to the Landlord relating to the accounting year in question ("the relevant year").

- a copy of the audited accounts signed by the auditor as a true and fair representation of the Tenant's accounts and records relating to the Property

- a schedule of all the leases, licences and occupational interests deriving out of the Property and current at the end of that year, stating the date on which each one was granted, the period for which it was granted, the name of the tenant or licensee, the annual fee payable and any other information reasonably required by the Landlord.

6.   **The audit certificate**

Every audit certificate must show the following:

(a)   the ground rent percentage

(b)   the rent payable for the accounting year preceding the relevant year

(c)   the gross income from the buildings on the Property for the relevant year

(d)   the difference between the payments on account for the relevant year and the rent payable for the relevant year; and

(e)   the rent calculation.

7.   **Differences and disputes**

Differences or disputes relating to this schedule or the calculation of gross income are to be resolved in accordance with the dispute resolution clause in this lease.

EXECUTED AS A DEED)

by affixing the common seal of)

)

in the presence of:)

Authorised officer

EXECUTED as a DEED by   )

LIMITED   )

acting by a director in the presence of:)

                                        Director

Witness signature..

Witness name (printed)......................................

Witness address..

....

Witness occupation..

FLAT LEASE

There follows a template for the long-term lease of a flat granted at a premium with a nominal rent, and including a service charge. It will have to be varied, for example to include a garage or parking space, or to cope with the vagaries of the building or its grounds.

As before, the prescribed clauses are fully integrated

DATED

[► *Insert name of landlord*]

-and-

[► *Insert name of tenant*]

LEASE OF FLAT

at

[► *Insert address of property*]

► Smith Brown & Co

118 High Street

Anytown

Flintshire AB6 8PX

Ref:►

LR1. Date of lease	20▶
LR2. Title number(s)	**LR2.1 Landlord's title number(s)** *Title number(s) out of which this lease is granted. Leave blank if not registered.* ▶ **LR2.2 Other title numbers** *Existing title number(s) against which entries of matters referred to in LR9, LR10, LR11 and LR13 are to be made* ▶
LR3. Parties to this lease *Give full names, addresses and company's registered number, if any, of each of the parties. For Scottish companies use a SC prefix and for limited liability partnerships use an OC prefix. For foreign companies give territory in which incorporated.*	**Landlord** ▶ **Tenant** ▶ **Other parties** ▶ *Specify capacity of each party, for example "management company", "guarantor", etc*
LR4. Property *Insert a full description of the land being leased* *Where there is a letting of part of a registered title, a plan must be attached to this lease and any floor levels must be specified.*	**In the case of a conflict between this clause and the remainder of this lease then, for the purposes of registration, this clause shall prevail.** The ▶[insert] floor flat known as ▶[address including postcode if known] coloured pink on the attached plan ▶[together with the garden area also coloured pink on the plan] [together with the store on the ▶[insert] floor of the building shown coloured yellow on the plan]
LR5. Prescribed statements etc	NONE
LR6. Term for which the Property is leased	The term is as follows:
LR7. Premium *Insert a full description of the land being leased*	▶
LR8. Prohibitions or restrictions on disposing of this lease	This lease contains a provision that prohibits or restricts dispositions.

LR9. Rights of acquisition etc *Insert the relevant provisions in the sub-clauses or refer to the clause, schedule or paragraph of a schedule in this lease which contains the provisions*	**LR9.1 Tenant's contractual rights to renew this lease, to acquire the reversion or another lease of the Property, or to acquire an interest in other land** NONE **LR9.2 Tenant's covenant to (or offer to) surrender this lease** NONE **LR9.3 Landlord's contractual rights to acquire this lease** NONE
LR10. Restrictive covenants given in this lease by the Landlord in respect of land other than the Property *Insert the relevant provisions or refer to the clause, schedule or paragraph of a schedule in this lease which contains the provisions.*	NONE
LR11. Easements *Refer here only to the clause, schedule or paragraph of a schedule in this lease which sets out the easements*	**LR11.1 Easements granted by this lease for the benefit of the Property** SCHEDULE 1 **LR11.2 Easements granted by this lease over the Property for the benefit of other property** SCHEDULE 2
LR12. Estate rent charge burdening the Property	NONE
LR13. Application for standard form of restriction *Set out the full text of the standard form of restriction and the title against which it is to be entered. If you wish to apply for more than one standard form of restriction use this clause to apply for each of them, tell us who is applying against which title and set out the full text of the restriction you are applying for.* *Standard forms of restriction are set out in Schedule 4 to the Land Registration Rules 2003*	NONE

1.   **INTERPRETATION**

(1)   **General**

The following provisions apply throughout this lease.

(2)   **LR clauses**

Clauses LR 1 to LR 14 contain definitions, descriptions and explanations that apply throughout this lease. In particular "the Property" is defined in clause LR4 and "the term" in clause LR6.

(3)   **Meaning of "the building"**

"The building" is the structure containing the Property.

(4)   **Gender and number**

Words of one gender include all other genders, and the singular includes the plural and vice versa.

(5)   **Joint and several benefit and liability**

Where a party consists of more than one person, the rights and obligations of that party under this lease are rights and obligations of those persons separately, together or in combination.

(6)   **Corporations**

A person includes a company or other body corporate.

(7)   **Obligations**

Any of the tenant's obligations not to do something includes an obligation not to allow that thing to be done by another person.

(8)   **Amendment or repeal of statutes**

(a)   Reference to a repealed Act of Parliament is a reference to the Act which, with or without modification, replaces or corresponds to the repealed Act.

(b)   Reference to an Act of Parliament which has been amended is a reference to that Act as amended.

(9)   **Successors in title**

The Landlord includes the person who, at any particular time, owns the immediate reversion on this lease. The Tenant includes the person who, at any particular time, is given the right by the lease to possess the Property.

2.   **PREMIUM**

The Landlord acknowledges receipt of the sum specified in clause LR7 paid by the Tenant as premium for this lease.

3.   **GRANT**

(1)   The Landlord leases the Property to the Tenant for the term.

(2)   This lease carries with it the rights for all purposes associated with the Property set out in schedule 1. Those rights are exercisable in common with all persons having the same or similar rights.

(3)   The Landlord excepts from this lease the main structural parts of the building and those other parts which the Landlord is liable to repair, renew or redecorate under this lease.

(4)   The Landlord reserves from this lease the rights set out in schedule 2.

4.   **RENT AND OTHER PAYMENTS BY TENANT**

(1)   **Rent**

(a)   The Tenant agrees to pay the rent of £10 a year in advance to the Landlord without deduction or set-off.

(b)   The first payment (apportioned if necessary) is to be made on the date of this lease and all subsequent payments are to be made on 1 January each year of the term.

(2)   **Service charge**

The Tenant will pay the Landlord a service charge in accordance with schedule 3.

(3)   **Council tax and other outgoings**

The Tenant must pay all council tax, rates, taxes and outgoings that are now or at any time during the term charged, assessed or imposed upon the Property or upon the owner or occupier of it.

5.   **MAINTENANCE, REPAIR AND ALTERATION OF THE PROPERTY**

(1)   **Maintaining the interior**

(a)   The Tenant must keep in proper repair and condition (and where necessary, replace) the following parts of the Property:

- the interior;
- all non-structural walls wholly within the Property;
- all ceilings, plasterboards and other ceiling finishes (but not the timbers or other structural elements upholding any ceiling);
- all floors and floorboards, floor tiles and other floor finishes including (in the case of concrete floors) the screed finishes but not the joists, concrete slab or other substructure supporting floors;
- all doors, door frames, door fittings and door furniture; windows and window frames; and all glass in windows and doors;
- the toilet facilities and the water, sanitary and heating apparatus and all sewers and drains and gas pipes and mains which solely serve the Property;
- the light fittings and other electrical fittings and all electricity cables, mains and wiring which solely serve the Property; and
- additions and improvements to the Property and the fixtures to it.

(b)   The Tenant's obligation under paragraph 0 does not extend to—

- any part of the building which falls within the Landlord's obligations, or
- damage caused by any insured risk unless the insurance money is irrecoverable through an act or default of the Tenant, his family or anyone on his behalf.

(2)   **Care of the interior**

(a)   In every fifth year of the term and in the last three months of the term (however this lease comes to an end) the Tenant must—

- clean, prepare and paint in a workmanlike manner (with two coats of appropriate good quality paint) the walls, woodwork, metalwork and other parts of the interior of the Property previously or usually painted; and, with every such painting,
- varnish, emulsion, wash, stop, whiten, colour and paper in a proper manner the parts which are usually dealt with in that way.

(b)   In the last year of the term, the colours and patterns must first be approved by the Landlord in writing.

(3)   **Works and consents required by law and compliance with statutory directions**

(a)   The Tenant must comply with all statutes, regulations, orders, statutory instruments and byelaws whether made before or after the date of this lease and with all lawful directions and requirements of any public authority in respect of the Property or the Tenant's occupation or use of the Property.

(b)   The Tenant must carry out all works required in respect of the Property or under statutes, regulations, orders, statutory instruments and byelaws whether made before or after the date of this lease.

(c)   The Tenant must obtain all approvals, consents and permissions (including planning permission) required by the law in respect of the Property or the Tenant's use of the Property.

(d)   Nothing in this clause requires the Tenant to carry out any works which are within the scope of the Landlord's obligations under this lease.

(4)   **Alterations, additions and damage**

(a)   The Tenant must not make any alterations or additions to the structure of the Property or building without first obtaining—

•   the consent of the Landlord (and that consent may be granted or withheld at the discretion of the Landlord) and

•   any planning permission or building consent which may be required.

(b)   The Tenant must comply with all conditions of those permissions and consents to the reasonable satisfaction of the Landlord.

(c)   The Tenant must not vandalise the Property, or deliberately or carelessly allow the Property to deteriorate.

(d)   The Tenant must make good any damage caused to the Property, the building or other properties in the building by the act or default of the Tenant, the Tenant's family, or an agent or visitor of the Tenant.

(5)   **Condition of the Property at the end of the lease**

At the termination of this lease (however it ends) the Tenant must vacate the Property and hand it back to the Landlord together with all fixtures, fittings and things which were in the Property at the start of this lease or have, at any time, been fixed to the Property during the term (tenant's fixtures excepted) in proper repair and condition and decorated and repaired in accordance with this lease.

(6)   [▶ **Boundaries**

The Tenant will maintain (and where necessary, erect or plant) to the satisfaction of the Landlord the fence, wall or hedge along the boundaries of the Property marked with an inward-facing T on the attached plan.]

6.   MAINTENANCE AND REPAIR OF BUILDING AND SURROUNDS

(1)   The Landlord will repair and where necessary renew the structure and the exterior of the building, including—

(a)   the roof, including roof insulation

(b)   the foundations

(c)   external walls

(d)   interior structural walls, but not the interior surface of any wall bounding the rooms of the Property or the surface of any interior structural wall

(e)   timbers, joists, beams and structural slabs

(f)   chimney stacks, drains, gutters and down pipes

(g)   the pipes, wires, cables and sewers which provide services to the building

(h)   any boilers and heating apparatus serving the building, but not the heating apparatus exclusively for the Property

(i)   any lift, lift shaft or machinery

(j)   any walls or fences within the grounds of the building, except any which are marked with an inward-facing T on the attached plan.

(2)   In addition, the Landlord will redecorate and keep in good order the exterior of the building.

(3)   The Landlord will also—

(a)   keep the common areas of the building adequately lit and decorated

(b)   maintain the floor coverings of those common areas

(c)   tend, tidy and maintain the gardens, forecourts, paths and drives adjacent to the building and used in connection with it, so far as these are still the property of the Landlord.

(4)   The Landlord is not liable to the tenant for any breach of this clause unless the Landlord fails to carry out the work within a reasonable period after the Tenant has given the Landlord notice of the breach.

7.   INSURANCE

(1)   The Landlord will insure the building with a reputable insurer against loss or damage by the insured risks (see below) in the sum which represents the full reinstatement cost, plus a reasonable sum for professional fees and other incidental costs.

(2)   The insured risks are fire, lightning, explosion, earthquake, landslip, subsidence, heave, riot, civil commotion, terrorism, impact from aircraft and aerial devices, storm, flood, impact by vehicles, damage by malicious persons and vandals, and other risks which the Landlord from time to time reasonably considers should be covered.

(3)   The Landlord's obligation under this clause excludes all property of the Tenant, which is the Tenant's responsibility to insure.

(4)   The Landlord need not maintain a separate policy of insurance for the building but may insure by a block or general policy.

(5)   The Landlord will lay out all money received in respect of its insurance (except sums in respect of professional fees) in rebuilding or reinstating that part of the building destroyed or damaged, including other flats in the building.

(6)   The Tenant may inspect the Landlord's insurance policy during normal office hours if he gives the Landlord at least seven days notice.

8.   SUSPENSION OF PAYMENTS IF PROPERTY DAMAGED OR DESTROYED BY INSURED RISKS

(1)   If the Property is destroyed or so damaged by any of the insured risks as to be unfit for occupation and use then, subject to paragraph 0, the rent and service charge (or a fair proportion according to the nature and extent of the damage sustained) will

be suspended until the Property, in the reasonable opinion of the Landlord, is again fit for occupation and use.

(2)   But this does not apply if—

(a)   the Property is destroyed or damaged by the act, default or negligence of the Tenant, or of the Tenant's agents or visitors; or

(b)   the Landlord's insurance has been invalidated, or payment of the policy money refused in whole or in part, in consequence of some act or default of the Tenant or the tenant's agents or visitors.

(3)   Disputes about the effect of this clause are to be decided by arbitration.

9.   USE OF THE PROPERTY

(1)   **Permitted use**

The Tenant may use the Property only as one self-contained residential unit in the occupation of one family.

(2)   **Further restrictions on use of the Property**

The Tenant must not use the Property for—

(a)   an illegal or immoral act or purpose

(b)   a sale by auction

(c)   the sale of intoxicating liquor, or

(d)   the storage of trade goods or for the trade of materials.

This does not limit the scope of subclause (1).

(3)   **Use affecting insurance policies**

The Tenant must not do anything on the Property which might invalidate any insurance policy taken out by the Landlord in respect of the building, or in respect of any adjoining or neighbouring premises of the Landlord, or which might cause an increase in the premium charged for that insurance.

(4)   **Damage or injury arising from the Tenant's use of the Property**

The Tenant must keep the Landlord entirely clear from (that is, indemnified against) losses, claims and expense arising directly or indirectly from—

(a)   the Tenant's use and occupation of the Property

(b)   the act, omission, negligence or default of the Tenant (or of the agents or visitors of the Tenant), or

(c)   breach by the tenant of the terms of this lease.

10.   ACTIVITIES IN THE PROPERTY AND BUILDING

(1)   **Receiving dishes and other apparatus**

Except with the written consent of the Landlord, the Tenant must not fix to the Property or to the building a television or radio aerial or dish, or other apparatus.

(2)   **Common areas**

The Tenant must not place or leave in a common area of the building (including any lift) furniture, cycles, prams, toyboxes, rubbish or other obstruction. The Tenant must not allow any garden area which the Tenant has a right to use under this lease to be occupied or part occupied for storage of goods or materials.

(3)   **Roof space**

(a)   The Tenant must not enter any roof space above the Property.

(b)   But this does not apply if the Tenant first obtains the Landlord's consent and the entry is to carry out work which the tenant is responsible for under this lease.

(4)   **Meter cupboards**

The Tenant must not enter the Landlord's meter cupboards in the building, but this does not affect the rights of entry of the supply companies to their meters.

(5)   **Flower boxes and the like**

(a)   The Tenant must not place or expose outside the Property above ground floor level any flower box, pot or other article.

(b)   The Tenant must not shake or throw any matter or article out of any door or window of the Property.

(6)   **Nuisance and the like**

The Tenant must not in the Property, the building or the grounds of the building do anything which is or might tend to be a nuisance or annoyance, cause of disturbance or cause of damage to the Landlord or to any occupier of property nearby.

(7)   **Harassment**

The Tenant must not in the Property, the building or the grounds of the building harass any individual on account of his or her race or for any other reason.

(8)   **Floorcoverings**

(a)   The Tenant must cover all the floors of the Property with carpet.

(b)   But in the kitchen and bathroom all-over cork, rubber or vinyl sheet or tiles, or some other noise-deadening material may be used instead.

(9)   **Blockages**

(a)   The Tenant must not place or leave in the sinks, baths, lavatories or pipes of the Property any rags, dirt, rubbish or similar substance.

(b)   The Tenant must not allow any blockage to the drains, sinks or baths of the Property.

(c)   The Tenant must take precautions to protect pipes against freezing.

(10)   **Animals**

The Tenant must not keep in the Property any animal or bird except a domestic pet.

(11)   **Lifts**

The Tenant must not overload the lift.

(12)   **Gas safety checks**

At least once a year, the Tenant must have all gas appliances in the Property tested for safety by an approved gas inspector. The tenant must make the inspection certificate available to the Landlord on request.

11.   **ASSIGNMENTS AND CHARGES**

(1)   **Registration**

Within one month of an assignment or charge of this lease by means of a document, the Tenant must send a copy of the document to the Landlord and pay the Landlord's reasonable charges for the registration.

(2)   **Devolution on death**

In the case of death, the document is the grant of probate or letters of administration and the one month period begins with the issue of the grant.

(3)   **Meaning of assignment**

In this clause, "assignment" means a disposal of the whole or part of the Property for the residue of the term or for a term of more than 21 years, and includes devolution on death.

12.   INSPECTIONS AND REPAIRS

(1)   **Entry to examine property and exercise rights**

(a)   The Tenant must permit the Landlord, its employees or agents, and others authorised by the Landlord, on reasonable notice (except in an emergency) to enter the Property—

- to examine its state and condition

- to examine how it is being used, or

- to exercise any of the Landlord's rights under this lease.

(b)   The Landlord must make good the damage to the Property caused by that entry and work.

(2)   **Notice to repair**

(a)   Within three months of a notice given by the Landlord (or sooner if the nature of the works requires it) the Tenant must carry out all works for which the Tenant is liable under this lease and which are referred to in the notice.

(b)   If within three months of that notice the Tenant does not start and diligently carry out the works, then the Tenant must allow the Landlord, its employees or agents and others authorised by the Landlord to enter the Property and carry out the works. The Tenant must pay the whole cost of the works to the Landlord within fourteen days of a demand.

(3)   **Entry to repair and renew building**

(a)   The Tenant will allow the Landlord, its employees and agents, and others authorised by the Landlord at all reasonable times on prior notice (except in an emergency) to enter the Property to repair the building or to carry out any other works for the benefit of the building or the Property.

(b)   The Landlord must make good the damage to the Property caused by that entry and work.

(4)   **Boards for sale or reletting**

(a)   During the six months before the end of the term the Tenant must allow the Landlord to fix and retain reasonable-size notice boards to conspicuous parts of the Property announcing that the Property is to be let or disposed of.

(b)   At all reasonable times of the day during that period the Tenant must permit all persons authorised by the Landlord to enter and view the Property.

13.   ENFORCEMENT OF OBLIGATIONS AGAINST NEIGHBOURS

(1)   If the Tenant requires the Landlord in writing, the Landlord will enforce the obligations of a lessee of any other flat in the building.

(2)   The Tenant must first indemnify the landlord against all costs and expenses, and provide whatever security for costs and expenses the Landlord reasonably requires.

14.   TENANT'S COVENANTS NOT AFFECTED BY DEALINGS WITH NEIGHBOURS

The obligations in this lease on the Tenant are not affected or compromised by any variation (whether temporary or permanent) of similar obligations on neighbours.

15.   RESERVATION OF LANDLORD'S POSITION

(1)   The Landlord has no greater duty towards the Tenant or to the building than the common duty of care.

(2)   The Landlord is not liable to the tenant where any services to the building are interrupted by—

    (a)   necessary maintenance or repair, or

    (h)   anything beyond the landlord's control, such as

        •   damage by fire or water

        •   mechanical breakdown

        •   frost or other inclement weather

        •   unavoidable shortage of fuel, materials, water or labour.

(3)   The Landlord is not liable to the tenant for any act or omission of any employee of the Landlord in the performance or purported performance of any duty relating to the services to the building.

(4)   This lease does not confer on the Tenant any easement, privilege or right except those set out in schedule 1.

16.   LANDLORD'S RIGHT TO USE ADJOINING OR NEIGHBOURING LAND AND BUILDINGS

(1)   The Landlord is entitled to deal as it thinks fit with adjoining or neighbouring property of the Landlord and to erect, or have erected a building on that adjoining or neighbouring property, whether that building does or does not affect or diminish the light or air enjoyed by the Property.

(2)   Nothing in this lease imposes a restriction on the use of any land or building not included in this lease. Nor does the Tenant have any standing in relation to the grant, enforcement, release or modification of the property or rights of any tenant or licensee of the Landlord relating to land or buildings not included in this lease.

17.   NOTICES

(1)   **What are notices**

In this clause, a notice includes a consent, request, approval, demand and notification, as well as the account under schedule 3.

(2)   **Writing required**

Any notice under this lease must be given in writing.

(3)   **Timing of delivery**

Notices are to be taken as received in accordance with the following table.

Mode	Received
Hand	On delivery
First class post*	Two working days after posting
Recorded delivery	On the day of posting
Fax before 3pm	On the day of sending
Fax at 3pm or later	On the next working day

* See subclause (4) below

(4)   **Returned post**

A notice sent by first class post but returned undelivered is not sufficiently served under this lease.

(5)   **Address for service**

Notices given to the persons in the left hand column below are served if left at or sent to an address in the right hand column opposite.

Recipient	Address for service
Individual landlord	The Landlord's address given in this lease; or the Landlord's address for service most recently notified to the Tenant.
Company landlord	The Landlord's registered office; or the Landlord's address for service most recently notified to the Tenant.
Individual tenant	The Property; or the Tenant's last known address or place of business in the United Kingdom
Company tenant	The Tenant's registered office; or the Property

(6)   **Email not service**

Sending by email does not constitute good service under this lease.

18.   RE-ENTRY AND FORFEITURE

(1)   A forfeiting event occurs within the meaning of this clause if—

(a)   the rent or any other sum payable by the tenant under this lease is in arrears and unpaid for twenty one days after becoming payable (whether formally demanded or not) or

(b)   there is any breach by the Tenant of any of the Tenant's obligations in this lease.

(2)   Whenever a forfeiting event occurs, the Landlord may re-enter the Property at any time and this lease then comes to an end.

(3)   This right arises even if a previous right of re-entry has been waived.

(4)   The ending of this lease under this clause does not affect the rights of either party in relation to any breach of the terms of this lease which occurred before this lease ended.

19. **COSTS OF SERVICE OF NOTICES AND THE LIKE**

The Tenant must pay the Landlord on demand the expenses (including legal costs and surveyors' fees) incurred by the Landlord which arise from, or are incidental to—

(1) the preparation and service of a notice under section 146 of the Law of Property Act 1925;

(2) the contemplation of taking of proceedings under sections 146 and 147 of that Act whatever the outcome of those proceedings;

(3) the preparation and service of notices and schedules relating to the condition of the Property, whether served before or after this lease has ended;

(4) the abatement of a nuisance in the Property, and the execution of all works necessary for abating any nuisance at the Property in obedience to a notice served by a public authority; and

(5) an application by the Tenant to the Landlord for a consent required by virtue of this lease.

20. **CONTRACTS (RIGHTS OF THIRD PARTIES) ACT 1999**

A person who is not a party to this lease has no right to enforce any of its terms.

21. **QUIET ENJOYMENT**

The Landlord agrees with the Tenant that, provided the Tenant punctually pays the rent and observes the Tenant's obligations, the Tenant may peaceably use the property without any interruption by the Landlord or by anyone claiming under or in trust for the Landlord.

22. **THIS LEASE A DEED**

The parties have entered into this lease as a deed.

SCHEDULE 1

Rights granted with this lease

1. **Access**

(a) The right of passage on foot over the access ways coloured ▶ [blue] on the attached plan.

(b) The right of passage with private vehicles over the driveway coloured blue and hatched ▶ [black] on that plan, but not the right to park or store vehicles there.

(c) The right of access to the Property over the common areas of the building (including any lift) and the gardens, forecourts, drives and pathways in the grounds of the building.

2. **Services**

(a) The right to passage and running of services to and from the Property through the sewers, drains, pipes, wires, conduits, ducts, cables and other similar devices ("conducting media") now or at any time during the term laid over the adjoining land of the Landlord.

(b) The right in paragraph (a) carries with it the right of entry to the land in or over which those services run at reasonable hours and on giving reasonable notice (except in an emergency, when no notice need be given) for the purpose of inspecting, cleaning, repairing or renewing the conducting media. The person entering must create as little interference and disturbance as possible, and as soon as practicable make good the damage caused.

3. **Support**

The right to support and protection to the Property as now enjoyed from the building.

4. **Benefit of obligations**

The benefit of any obligation entered into with the Landlord by the owners of other flats in the building, but only so far as those obligations are intended to benefit the Property or the Tenant and the benefit can in law accrue to the Tenant.

5.   **Disposal of refuse**

(a)   For the disposal of domestic refuse from the Property, the right to place in the communal dustbin store coloured ▶[green] on the attached plan one domestic size wheelie bin or other container approved by the local authority for household use.

(b)   The right to use of the communal rubbish chute coloured ▶[orange] on the attached plan for the disposal of domestic refuse from the Property.

6.   **Clothes drying**

The right to use for domestic washing the communal drying area coloured ▶[purple] on the attached plan and the clothes-drying facility provided there by the Landlord.

7.   **▶[Gardens**

Use of the garden area coloured ▶[*insert colour*] on the plan.]

SCHEDULE 2

Rights reserved by the Landlord

1. **Services**

    The right to uninterrupted passage and running of services for
    the building through the sewers, drains, pipes, wires, conduits,
    ducts, cables and other similar devices ("conducting media") in the
    Property now or at any time during the term.

2. **Conducting media**

    The right to construct or maintain in the Property any conducting
    media for services to or from any part of the building or adjoining
    land of the Landlord.

3. **Support and other easements**

    (a) The right of support and protection to the building as is now or at any
    time during the term enjoyed from the Property.

    (b) The rights to light, air, shelter and other benefits now or at any time
    during the term enjoyed by all nearby land owned by the Landlord.

4. **Access to adjoining property**

    A right of way on foot for the Landlord and its successors in title as
    owners and occupiers for the time being of the adjoining property
    number ▶ [*insert number*] over the part of the property coloured pink
    hatched black on the attached plan.

5. **Communal TV system**

    (a) The right to deal with the communal TV system for the building
    which passes through the Property, and to receive and transmit
    through that system.

    (b) To "deal with" includes to place, maintain, repair, renew, disconnect
    and remove.

SCHEDULE 3

Service charge

1. **What the service charge is**

   The service charge is ▶ [*insert figure*] % of (C + R) where—

   C = the costs incurred by the landlord on the actions, activities and items set out in paragraph 2; and

   R = the reserve under paragraph 4(d).

2. **Landlord's heads of expenditure which form the basis for the service charge**

(a) Renewals, repairs and insurance

   Fulfilment of the Landlord's obligations under clause 0 (maintenance and repair of building and surrounds) and clause 0 (insurance).

(b) Heating

   Periodic inspection, overhaul, repair and (when necessary) replacement of any central heating or hot water system serving the Property and any other property in the building.

(c) Lifts

   Periodic inspection, overhaul, repair and (when necessary) replacement of any lift, lift shaft or lift machinery in the building.

(d) Fuel

   Oil, gas, electricity or other fuel for the boilers serving the building and for the lifts in the building.

(e) Common areas

   Carpeting, re-carpeting, floor covering, cleaning, decorating and lighting the common areas of the building; and cleaning the windows in the common areas.

(f) Common services

   Making, repairing, maintaining, rebuilding and cleaning all paths, roads, pipes, drains, watercourses walls or other amenities belonging to or used for the building.

(g)   Outgoings

Any charges, assessments and outgoings payable by the Landlord in relation to the building.

(h)   Administration costs

Preparing the annual accounts, and the procedures and audits in support of them, the management of the building and the overheads ancillary to management.

(i)   Gardens

Upkeep of the gardens forecourts and paths used in connection with the building.

(j)   Statutory process

Taking all steps which the Landlord considers expedient to comply with or contest the incidence of any statutory process relating to the building and to which the Tenant is not directly liable, in particular relating to—

- town and country planning
- public health
- highways or streets
- drainage
- supply of services.

(k)   Periodic Payments

Expenditure which periodically recurs (whether regular or not) and whenever it is disbursed (even it arose before the date of this lease).

3.   **Advance payments of service charge**

(a)   To avoid payment by the Tenant of a substantial lump sum each year, the Tenant must pay the Landlord on every quarter day a contribution towards the service charge for that year.

(b)   The quarter days are 25 March, 24 June, 29 September and 25 December.

(c)   The quarterly payment is calculated by reference to the service charge payable by the Tenant in the preceding year. That figure is then divided by four. For example, if the total service charge for the preceding year was £1,200 then the quarterly payments for the next year would be £300.

(d)   The contribution for the year in which this lease is granted is a reasonable estimate by the Landlord of the service charge payable by the Tenant for that year.

(e)   The first payment of contribution will be apportioned to the period beginning with the date of this lease and will be payable in arrears on the following quarter day.

4.   Preparation of account

(a)   As soon as possible after the end of the Landlord's financial year, the Landlord must prepare an account and serve it on the Tenant.

(b)   The Landlord's financial year is the period beginning on ▶ [1 April each year and ending on 31 March of the next year], or any other annual period which—

•   the Landlord may from time to time decide, or

•   according to law may be the period in which the accounts of the Landlord are made up, either generally or in relation to the building.

(c)   The purpose of the account is to fix the service charge payable by the Tenant, and to demonstrate to the Tenant how much he has to pay.

(d)   In addition to the expenditure envisaged by paragraph 2, the Landlord may at its discretion in any financial year add a reasonable provision for anticipated expenditure arising irregularly or less frequently than every year ("the reserve").

(e)   The account (or a copy certified by the person who prepared it) is conclusive evidence of the matters it covers.

5.   What the account must contain

(a)   The account must contain a summary of the Landlord's expenditure under paragraph 2 and the reserve for the year in question, with the relevant details and figures sharing how the total is made up.

(b)   The account must also show the amount payable by the Tenant as service charge, by applying the relevant percentage to the total.

(c)   The account must give credit for the advance payments made by the Tenant.

6. Payment following account

If the account shows a balance payable to the Landlord, the Tenant must pay it to the Landlord within fourteen days of receiving the account. If the account shows the Tenant in credit, the Landlord will carry it over to the following year.

7. Service charge if lease ends prematurely

If this lease ends prematurely the service charge provisions continue to apply, but only in relation to the actual term.

THE COMMON SEAL   )

of the Landlord was fixed   )

was fixed in the presence of:)

                                                       Director

                                        Director/company secretary

EXECUTED as a deed by the   )

Landlord acting by:)

                                                       Director

                                        Director/company secretary

SIGNED as a deed by   )

▶ [*name of tenant*]   )

in the presence of:)

WITNESS

Name:

Address:

Occupation:

PLAYING FIELD LEASE

This is a lease of a playing field by charity trustees whose title is unregistered in favour of a parish council. No rent is payable, and responsibility for control, repair and management is devolved to the council. There is a mower shed on the field (see clause 8.1 (f)). Accordingly (and like all precedents in this book) it will need to be adapted for the circumstances of the particular transaction.

▶ PLAYING FIELD TRUST

to

▶PARISH COUNCIL

LEASE

of

PLAYING FIELD

at

▶

LR1. Date of lease	2020
LR2. Title number(s)	**LR2.1 Landlord's title number(s)** NONE **LR2.2 Other title numbers** ▶
LR3. Parties to this lease *Give full names, addresses and company's registered number, if any, of each of the parties. For Scottish companies use a SC prefix and for limited liability partnerships use an OC prefix. For foreign companies give territory in which incorporated*	**Landlord** ▶ trustees of the ▶ Playing Field Trust, charity number ▶ **Tenant** ▶ THE PARISH COUNCIL OF ▶ IN THE COUNTY OF ▶ c/o The Clerk to ▶Parish Council ▶ **Tenant** NONE
LR4. Property	**In the case of a conflict between this clause and the remainder of this lease then, for the purposes of registration, this clause shall prevail.** The playing field land adjoining ▶ at ▶ shown edged red on the attached plan
LR5. Prescribed statements etc	NONE
LR6. Term for which the Property is leased	The term is as follows: the period of twenty-five years beginning on the date of this lease
LR7. Premium	NONE
LR8. Prohibitions or restrictions on disposing of this lease	This lease contains a provision that prohibits or restricts dispositions.

LR9. Rights of acquisition etc.	LR9.1 Tenant's contractual rights to renew this lease, to acquire the reversion or another lease of the Property, or to acquire an interest in other land
	NONE
	LR9.2 Tenant's covenant to (or offer to) surrender this lease
	NONE
	LR9.3 Landlord's contractual rights to acquire this lease
	NONE
LR10. Restrictive covenants given in this lease by the Landlord in respect of land other than the Property	NONE
LR11. Easements	LR11.1 Easements granted by this lease for the benefit of the Property
	NONE
	LR11.2 Easements granted or reserved by this lease over the Property for the benefit of other property
	NONE
LR12. Estate rentcharge burdening the Property	NONE
LR13. Application for standard form of restriction	NONE
LR14. Declaration of trust where there is more than one person comprising the Tenant *If the Tenant is one person, omit or delete all the alternative statements.* *If the Tenant is more than one person, complete this clause by omitting or deleting all inapplicable alternative statements.*	NOT APPLICABLE

1. DEFINITIONS

1.1 Clauses LR 1 to LR 14 contain some definitions, descriptions and explanations of words used in this lease. "The Property" is defined in clause LR 4 and "the term" is defined in clause LR 6. In addition, the following apply.

1.2 The expressions "landlord covenants" and "tenant covenants" have the same meanings as in the Landlord and Tenant (Covenants) Act 1995.

2. INTERPRETATION

2.1 Gender and number

Words of one gender include any other gender, and the singular includes the plural and vice versa.

2.2 Joint and several benefit and liability

Where a party consists of more than one person, the rights and obligations of that party under this lease are rights and obligations of those persons separately, all together or in any combination.

2.3 Corporations

A person includes a company or other body corporate.

2.4 Obligations

A Tenant's obligation not to do anything includes an obligation not to allow that thing to be done by another person.

3. LETTING

The Landlord lets the Property to the Tenant for the term subject to the exceptions and reservations in the schedule.

4. RENT AND PAYMENTS BY TENANT

4.1 Rent

No rent is payable under this lease.

4.2 Rates and other outgoings

The Tenant must pay all business rates, taxes and outgoings that are now or may at any time during the term be charged, assessed or imposed upon the Property or upon the owner or occupier of it, excluding any arising from the Landlord's ownership of the freehold of the Property. The Tenant must pay the appropriate authority direct.

4.3　**Costs of service of notices and for consents**

The Tenant must pay on demand all expenses (including solicitors' costs and surveyors' fees) incurred by the Landlord which arise from, or are incidental to—

(a)　the granting of consent by the Landlord under this lease

(b)　preparation and service of a notice under section 146 of the Law of Property Act 1925

(c)　contemplation or taking of proceedings under sections 146 and 147 of that Act whatever the outcome of those proceedings, and

(d)　preparation and service of notices and schedules relating to the condition of the Property, whether served before or within 9 months of the ending of this lease.

4.4　**Shared facilities**

The Tenant agrees to contribute a reasonable and proper proportion of the expense of repairing, maintaining and cleaning all drains and other things used by the occupier of the Property in common with occupiers of premises adjoining or nearby.

5.　**USE OF THE PROPERTY**

5.1　**Sole use**

The Tenant is to use the Property for the purposes of a playing field, physical training and recreation as may be expedient for the benefit of the inhabitants of the parish of ▶ in the County of ▶ and its immediate vicinity, without distinction of sex or of political or other opinions.

5.2　**Prohibition on other uses**

The Tenant must not use the Property for any other purpose.

5.3　**Dangerous materials**

The Tenant must not bring on to or store at the Property any article, substance or liquid of a specially combustible, inflammable radioactive or dangerous nature.

5.4　**Nuisance notice**

If the Landlord gives notice to the Tenant requiring the stopping of a nuisance, the Tenant must stop the nuisance immediately.

5.5 Encroachment and acquisition of rights

(a) The Tenant must take all reasonable steps to prevent a trespass upon the Property or the acquisition of any new right to light, right of way, right of drainage or other easement over, on or under the Property.

(b) The Tenant must give notice to the Landlord of any threatened trespass or attempt to acquire an easement or right of the kind referred to above as soon as the Tenant becomes aware of it.

(c) If requested by the Landlord, the Tenant must stop the trespass, acquisition of an easement or right of that kind.

(d) The Tenant must allow the Landlord (on reasonable notice except in an emergency) to enter the Property to do anything necessary to prevent an encroachment or acquisition of an easement or right.

5.6 Discharge into pipes and drains

(a) The Tenant must not discharge any oil, grease, acid or other noxious, toxic or corrosive substance into any pipe or drain serving the Property—

- which may cause an obstruction in, or damage to, any such pipe or drain; or

- to which any water or sewerage company or other competent authority may object.

(b) If any discharge occurs, the Tenant must immediately—

- make good any obstruction or damage to the satisfaction of the Landlord and the water or sewerage company or other competent authority; and

- comply with the reasonable requirements of the Landlord and the water or sewerage company or other competent authority to remedy the discharge or passage or to prevent its recurrence.

5.7 Damage or injury arising from the Tenant's use of the Property

The Tenant must protect (that is, indemnify) the Landlord against all losses, claims and expense arising directly or indirectly from—

(a)   the Tenant's use and occupation of the Property

(b)   an act, omission, negligence or default of the Tenant (or of the employees, agents, licensees or visitors of the Tenant), or

(c)   a breach by the Tenant of any of the terms of this lease.

5.8 Notices affecting the Property

If the Tenant receives a communication from a competent authority affecting or likely to affect the Property, the Tenant must—

(a)   immediately send details to the Landlord

(b)   without delay, take all reasonable steps to comply with the communication at the Tenant's expense, and

(c)   join with the Landlord in making any representation to the communicating authority reasonably required by the Landlord.

6. PLANNING REQUIREMENTS

6.1 Breach of planning control

The Tenant must not commit a breach of planning control.

6.2 Application for planning permission

(a)   Except with the written consent of the Landlord, the Tenant must not apply for planning permission to carry out any development at the Property or for change of use of the Property.

(b)   The Landlord may not unreasonably withhold its consent to apply for planning permission but it will always be reasonable for the Landlord to withhold consent if—

- the grant of the planning permission would have adverse implications for the Landlord, or

- grant of the planning permission might prejudice the restrictions on use in this lease.

(c)   In any event, the Tenant must supply the Landlord with—

- a copy of any application for planning permission

- a copy of any plans and other documents which the Landlord may reasonably require, and

- a copy of any planning permission granted to the Tenant.

6.3 **Works required by planning consent**

The Tenant must pay and satisfy any charge that may be imposed on breach by the Tenant of planning control or otherwise under the Town and Country Planning Act 1990.

6.4 **Works required by planning consent**

(a) Unless the Landlord directs otherwise, the Tenant must carry out during the term works to the Property required as a condition of any planning permission granted during the term.

(b) This applies whatever the date by which the works were stipulated to be carried out in the planning permission.

7. DEALINGS FORBIDDEN

7.1 The Tenant may not deal with this lease, nor (except in fulfilling its obligations under the use clause in this lease) give up or share possession or occupation of the Property or any part of it.

7.2 To "deal with" includes to assign, charge or underlet in whole or in part.

8. MAINTENANCE, REPAIR AND ALTERATION

8.1 **Maintaining the Property**

The Tenant must put and keep the whole Property in good condition. In particular the Tenant will—

   (a) cut the grass regularly

   (b) maintain and where necessary plant or replant trees

   (c) maintain the fences and hedges round the Property

   (d) drain the Property of surface and ground water

   (e) maintain the car park within the Property, the playground and the fixed equipment

   (f) repair the mower shed (known as and referred to in this lease as "the garage") and keep it in good condition. The garage is shown coloured yellow on the attached plan.

8.2 **Notice and entry to repair**

(a) Within twenty eight days from the date of a notice given by the Landlord (or sooner if the nature of the works requires it) the Tenant must carry out all works for which the Tenant is liable under this lease and which are referred to in the notice.

(b)   If within twenty eight days of that notice the Tenant does not start and diligently carry out the works, then the Tenant must allow the Landlord, its employees or agents and others authorised by the Landlord to enter the Property and carry out the works. The Tenant must pay the whole cost of the works to the Landlord within fourteen days of a demand.

8.3   **Works and consents required by law and compliance with statutory directions**

(a)   The Tenant must comply with all statutes, regulations, orders, statutory instruments and byelaws whether made before or after the date of this lease and with all lawful directions and requirements of any local or public authority in respect of the Property or the Tenant's occupation or use of the Property.

(b)   The Tenant must carry out all works required in respect of the Property by or under statutes, regulations, orders, statutory instruments and byelaws whether made before or after the date of this lease.

(c)   The Tenant must obtain all approvals, consents and permissions (including planning permission) required by law in respect of the Property or the Tenant's use of the Property.

8.4   **Alterations and additions to the Property**

(a)   The Tenant must not make an alteration or addition to the Property without first obtaining—

•   the consent of the Landlord in its role as landlord as opposed to its function as local or planning authority (and that consent may be granted or withheld at the discretion of the Landlord) and

•   any planning permission or building consent which may be required.

(b)   The Tenant must comply with all conditions of those permissions and consents to the reasonable satisfaction of the Landlord.

(c)   Before vacating the Property, the Tenant must (unless expressly released from this obligation) remove all alterations or additions and reinstate the Property to the satisfaction of the Landlord.

8.5   Condition of the Property at the end of the lease

At the end of the term the Tenant must vacate the Property and hand it back to the Landlord (together with all fixtures except tenant's fixtures) in the state which this lease requires the Tenant to keep it.

9.   INSPECTIONS AND VIEWINGS

9.1   During the term

The Tenant must permit the Landlord, its employees or agents, and others authorised by the Landlord, on reasonable notice (except in an emergency) to enter the Property to examine its condition and how it is being used and to exercise any of the rights granted to the Landlord by this lease.

9.2   Making good

The Landlord must make good all damage to the Property and tenant's fixtures caused by an entry.

10.   INSURANCE

10.1   Cover by Tenant

The Tenant will take out insurance with a reputable insurer against the following risks:

(a)   liability or damage caused by plant or machinery at the Property

(b)   liability to the public for personal injury or death caused by an accident or other incident at the Property

(c)   damage to any fixture, tree, plant or other asset on the Property.

10.2   Reinstatement

The Tenant will reinstate any asset for which the Tenant receives the money from its insurer.

10.3   Production of policy

The Tenant will produce its policy and the last premium receipt to the Landlord on request.

10.4   **Garage**

At the Landlord's expense, the Landlord will insure the garage to its full replacement value and will produce evidence of this to the Tenant on request.

11.   RE-ENTRY AND FORFEITURE

11.1   Each of the following is a forfeiting event within the meaning of this clause:

(a)   a sum payable by the Tenant under this lease is in arrears and unpaid for twenty-one days after becoming payable (whether formally demanded or not)

(b)   there is a breach by the Tenant of any of the tenant covenants in this lease.

11.2   If and whenever a forfeiting event occurs, the Landlord may re-enter the Property at any time and this lease then comes to an end. Re-entry on part is to be treated as re-entry on the whole.

11.3   This right arises even if a previous right of re-entry has been waived.

11.4   The ending of this lease under this clause does not affect the rights of any party in relation to any breach of the terms of this lease which occurred before this lease ended.

12.   TENANT'S COMPENSATION ON QUITTING

Subject to the provisions of section 38(2) of the Landlord and Tenant Act 1954, the Tenant is not entitled on vacating the Property to compensation under section 37 of that Act.

13.   LANDLORD'S NON-LIABILITY FOR ACCIDENTS ON THE PROPERTY

13.1   The Landlord is not responsible to the Tenant or to anyone on the Property for—

(a)   accident or injury on the Property, including injury resulting in death; and

(b)   damage or loss to an asset on the Property.

13.2   This does not apply to the extent that the accident, injury, damage or loss occurs as a result of negligence on the part of the Landlord.

14.   NOTICES

14.1   What is a notice

In this lease, a notice includes a consent, request, demand and notification.

14.2   Writing required

A notice under this lease must be given in writing.

14.3   Time of service

The notice will be taken to be received—

(a)   on delivery, if served by hand

(b)   two working days after posting if sent by ordinary first-class post, unless it is returned undelivered

(c)   on the day of sending, if sent by recorded delivery post

(d)   on the day sent by fax, if sent before 3pm

(e)   on the next working day after being sent by fax if sent at 3pm or later.

14.4   Email not service

Sending by email does not constitute good service under this lease.

14.5   Delivery of notice

(a)   A notice is taken to be delivered as follows:

- to the Landlord, if left at or sent to ▶; and

- to the Tenant, if left at or sent to the address for the Tenant in clause LR3 or to any other address for the Tenant set out in the Tenant's registered title to this lease.

(b)   These addresses are not mandatory, but are conclusive if adopted.

15.   DISPUTE RESOLUTION

15.1   Reference to arbitration

Unless a particular clause provides otherwise, a difference between the parties arising from this lease is to be referred to a single arbitrator under the Arbitration Act 1996.

15.2   **Appointment of arbitrator**

In the absence of agreement, any party may apply at any time to the President of the Royal Institution of Chartered Surveyors for the appointment of an arbitrator.

15.3   **Arbitrator unable to act**

If an appointed arbitrator dies or is incapable of acting, any party may apply to the President of the Royal Institution of Chartered Surveyors for the appointment of a new arbitrator.

15.4   **Reference to expert**

The preceding paragraphs do not apply if the parties agree in writing that an expert would better settle a particular difference.

15.5   **Referral back to arbitration**

If the parties cannot agree on an expert within one month of that agreement, the paragraphs relating to arbitration reapply to the difference.

15.6   **Expert's terms of employment**

The expert's conditions of appointment must include—

(a)   a requirement for the expert to consider any evidence or submissions made to him by the parties

(b)   power for the expert to make an order for costs binding on all parties, and

(c)   a provision that the expert's decision on questions of fact is binding on all parties.

16.   NO WARRANTY ON USE

16.1   Nothing in this lease or in any consent granted under this lease implies that the Property may be used for any particular purpose under the Town and Country Planning Act 1990.

16.2   Nothing in this lease is to be interpreted as a warranty by the Landlord on the fitness, stability, soundness or suitability of the Property for use by the Tenant as permitted by this lease.

16.3   The Landlord does not warrant that the facilities at the Property are fit for the purpose for which the Tenant intends to use the Property or for any particular purpose. Usage of the Property is at the Tenant's risk. The Landlord is not responsible for any loss, injury, damage or expense which the Tenant may incur if the Property or its facilities prove defective or unfit for any particular purpose.

16.4   This does not apply where statute or this lease make express provision otherwise.

17.   NO WAIVER OF COVENANTS

Each of the tenant covenants in this lease remains in full force even if the Landlord has—

17.1   temporarily waived or released another tenant covenant in this lease, or

17.2   varied, waived or released a similar covenant affecting premises belonging to the Landlord adjoining or nearby.

18.   QUIET ENJOYMENT

The Landlord agrees with the Tenant that, provided the Tenant observes the Tenant's obligations, the Tenant may peaceably use the Property without interruption by the Landlord or by anyone claiming under the Landlord.

19.   CONTRACTS (RIGHTS OF THIRD PARTIES) ACT 1999

A person who is not a party to this lease has no right to enforce any of its terms.

20.   RELEASE ON ASSIGNMENT OF REVERSION

On assignment of its reversion (however that happens) the Landlord is automatically released from the landlord covenants in this lease, regardless of the date a breach is alleged to have occurred.

21.   APPOINTMENT OF TRUSTEES

21.1   The individual persons comprising the Landlord are all the current trustees of the charitable trust known as the ▶   Playing Field Trust ("the Trust"). The Trust is registered with the Charity Commission under number ▶.

21.2   Deaths, resignations and appointments of trustees are properly recorded in the minutes of the Trust, but no deeds of appointment beyond those specified in clause 23 can be found.

22.   AUTHORITY TO LEASE

22.1   Under section 119 of the Charities Act 2011, the Landlord has obtained and considered a written report on the proposed disposition (namely this lease) dated ▶   from ▶   , a qualified surveyor instructed by the Landlord and acting exclusively for the Trust.

22.2   That report advised that it would not be in the best interests of the Trust to advertise the proposed disposition.

22.3   The trustees of the Trust have decided that they are satisfied, having considered the surveyor's report, that the terms of this lease are the best that can reasonably be obtained for the Trust.

23.   ACKNOWLEDGEMENT FOR PRODUCTION

The Landlord acknowledges the right of the Tenant to the production of the following documents, and to the supply of copies.

Date	Document	Parties

SCHEDULE

Exceptions and reservations

1. Interpretation

In this schedule—

"the pavilion" is the land and building retained by the Landlord adjoining the south side of the village hall, and shown coloured blue on the attached plan; and

"services" means electricity, telephone, gas, internet and water supplies; and foul and surface water drainage.

2. Access to the pavilion

The Landlord reserves a right of way with or without vehicles to and from the pavilion across the Property from the Street through the car park on the Property, but avoiding damage to any playing surface.

3. Services to the pavilion

The Landlord reserves the right to the supply of services under the surface of the Property to and from the pavilion, together with the ancillary rights to lay, repair and relay those services.

4. Repair of the pavilion

The Landlord reserves the right to enter the Property with workers and equipment to decorate, repair and replace the pavilion.

5. Repair of village hall

There is excepted from this lease the right for the owners and occupiers of the village hall to enter the Property with workers and equipment to decorate, repair and replace the village hall.

6. Exercise of these rights

The persons exercising the rights in this schedule must—

6.1   carry out any work as quickly and efficiently as possible;

6.2   avoid damage to the Property as far as they reasonably can; and

6.3   make good any damage to the Property without delay.

SIGNED as a DEED by)

)

in the presence of:)

Witness signature ....……………

Name of witness (printed) ....….………..

Address ....………………

....………………

....………………

Occupation ....….…………

EXECUTED AS A DEED by)

►   PARISH COUNCIL)

acting through councillors ► [*insert full*)

names of two councillors])

by the authority of a resolution of the Council)

dated   ►)

under reference ►   in the presence of:)

Witness signature ....……………

Name of witness (printed) ....….………..

Address ....………………

....………………

....………………

Occupation ....……………

EASY-IN-EASY-OUT LEASE

This lease is suitable where a landlord has a suite of offices or a light industrial estate which it proposes to let short-term on an easy-in-easy-out basis. The letting conditions are standard and might be created in PDF. All the variables are set out on the front page(s).

DATE: 20▶

TENANT: [*Insert tenant's FULL name and address - in the case of a company, set out its name, registered number and registered office address*]

GUARANTOR: [*State 'NONE' or insert guarantor's FULL name and address - in the case of a company, set out its name, registered number and registered office address*]

PROPERTY: Unit number ▶, [*insert address*] [▶coloured pink on the attached plan]

TERM: Three years beginning on ▶ [the date of this lease] [*or insert other date*]

RENT: ▶£   a year

RENT COMMENCEMENT DATE: ▶[The beginning of the term] [The date of this lease] [*or insert other date*]

RENT DEPOSIT: £ [▶ *insert figure or state 'NONE'*]

USE ALLOWED: ▶

This lease incorporates the letting conditions attached.

Where a guarantor is named above, condition 31 applies. Otherwise it does not.

Where a rent deposit figure is inserted above, schedule 4 applies. Otherwise it does not.

EXECUTED as a DEED by   )

▶   LIMITED)   Director

acting by its officers:)

…………………………………

Company secretary/Director

EXECUTED as a DEED by   )

▶   LIMITED)

………………………..

acting by a director in the presence of:)   Director

Witness signature ....……………

Name of witness (printed) ....…..………..

Address ....……………………..

...........................…………………………

...........................…………………………

Occupation ....………………

EXECUTED as a DEED by   )

▶   )

in the presence of:)

Witness signature ....……………

Name of witness (printed) ....…..………..

Address ....……………………..

...........................…………………………

...........................…………………………

Occupation ....………………

LETTING CONDITIONS

1.   LANDLORD

The Landlord under the lease is ▶ .

2.   INTERPRETATION

2.1   Terms on front page

The words and phrases defined or explained on page 1 and used in these conditions have the meanings assigned to them on page 1.

2.2   "The insured risks"

In addition, "the insured risks" are fire and such other risks as the Landlord may from time to time consider it desirable to insure against.

2.3   Gender, persons and number

Words importing one gender include both other genders; the singular includes the plural and vice versa: and reference to a person includes a company or other corporate body.

2.4   Joint and several benefits and burdens

Where a party consists of more than one person, the rights and obligations of those persons are enforceable by or against them separately, all together or in any combination.

2.5   Statutory references

References to a particular Act or statutory instrument are references to any amendment or re-enactment of it for the time being in force. But this provision does not apply to the Town and Country Planning (Use Classes) Order 1987.

3.   TENANT NOT TO ALLOW BREACHES

An obligation on the Tenant not to do anything includes an obligation not to cause it or allow it to be done by anyone else.

4.   LETTING

4.1   The Landlord lets the Property to the Tenant for the term, with the rights specified in schedule 1 of these conditions but excepting and reserving the rights specified in schedule 2.

4.2   No part of the forecourt adjacent to the Property is included in this letting.

5.   RENT PAYMENT

5.1   Beginning on the rent commencement date, the Tenant will pay the rent by equal instalments in advance on the first day of each month by direct debit and without deduction or set-off.

5.2   If payment starts or ends partway through a month, the rent will be apportioned.

6.   OTHER PAYMENTS

6.1   Outgoings

(a)   The Tenant will pay all business rates, sewerage rates, taxes, assessments, duties, impositions and outgoings whether parliamentary, local or otherwise now or later imposed or charged upon the Property or any part of it or on the owner, lessor, lessee or occupier of it.

(b)   This does not apply to income or capital taxes assessable on the Landlord in respect of rents and other payments arising under the lease or in respect of any consideration arising on any dealing (whether notional or actual) with the Landlord's interest in the Property.

(c)   The Tenant must promptly pay the appropriate authority direct. But where outgoings are assessed on the Property jointly with other premises, the Tenant must pay to the Landlord the proportion reasonably attributed to the Property by the Landlord.

6.2   Insurance proportion

The Tenant will repay to the Landlord on demand the sums which the Landlord from time to time pays by way of premiums in effecting or maintaining the insurance of the Property against the insured risks (defined in condition 2.2 above).

6.3   Gas, electricity, water and other supplies

The Tenant will pay to the suppliers all charges (including meter rents and appliance rentals) for gas, electricity, water, telephone and other services and supplies to the Property, and will observe all regulations and requirements of the suppliers.

6.4 Costs of lease

Unless the grant of the lease is a renewal in accordance with Part II of the Landlord and Tenant Act 1954, the Tenant will pay the Landlord's costs of and in connection with the preparation and completion of the lease.

6.5 Costs of notices

The Tenant will pay all expenses (including solicitors' costs and surveyors fees) incurred by the Landlord in and incidental to the preparation and service of—

(a) a notice under section 146 of the Law of Property Act 1925 or incurred in or in contemplation of proceedings under sections 146 and 147 of that Act even if forfeiture is avoided outside court action

(b) all notices and schedules relating to lack of repair of the Property whether the notices or schedules are served during or after the end of the lease.

6.6 VAT

The Tenant will pay all value added tax that may from time to time be charged on the rent or other sums payable by the Tenant under the lease.

6.7 Interest on late payments

If the Tenant fails to pay the rent or any other sum due under the lease, the Tenant must pay to the Landlord interest on all such sums at the rate of 4% above the base lending rate of the Landlord's bank for the time being from the date when that sum was due to the date on which it is actually paid.

6.8 Payments treated as rent

All payments due from the Tenant to the Landlord under the lease are to be treated and recoverable as rent

7. MAINTENANCE, DECORATION AND REPAIR: TENANT

7.1 Interior

The Tenant will keep the interior of the Property in repair and good condition (damage by the insured risks excepted) including all—

(a)   windows and glass,

(b)   lights, locks, latches, doors and door frames

(c)   electric, gas, water and sanitary apparatus and drains; and

(d)   landlord's fixtures.

7.2   **Painting**

(a)   The Tenant will prepare and paint in a proper manner with two coats of appropriate good quality paint all the walls, wood, iron and other parts of the interior of the Property previously or usually painted and with every such painting will grain, varnish, emulsion, wash, stop whiten and colour all such parts as are usually dealt with in that way.

(b)   The obligation in (a) arises—

- when the Landlord reasonably considers it necessary in order to maintain a high standard of decorative finish and attractiveness and to preserve the Property, but

- in any event in the last six months of the term however the term comes to an end.

7.3   **Inspection**

The Tenant will permit the Landlord or its agents and all others on reasonable notice to enter any part of the Property to examine its state and condition and its actual use.

7.4   **Notice to repair**

(a)   Within one month of a notice given by the Landlord (or sooner if the nature of the works requires it) the Tenant will execute all repairs and works for which the Tenant is liable under this lease and required by that notice.

(b)   If the Tenant does not with that period proceed with the execution of those repairs and works, then the Tenant will allow the Landlord or its agents with workmen, plant and equipment to enter any part of the Property and carry out those repairs and the Tenant will allow the Landlord or its agents with workmen, plant and equipment to enter any part of the Property and carry out those repairs and the Tenant will within 14 days of a request pay the cost of them to the Landlord.

8. MAINTENANCE AND REPAIR: LANDLORD

8.1 Main structure

The Landlord will maintain and keep in repair and good condition the main structure of the Property including—

(a) the foundations, load bearing walls and the roof

(b) the guttering and downpipes

(c) the tiles, slates or other roof coverings, and

(d) the external doors and window frames.

8.2 Exceptions

This obligation does not require the Landlord to carry out work—

(a) called for as a result of the Tenant's negligence or default, or of the negligence or default of another person on the Property with the express or implied consent of the Tenant;

(b) on or arising out of an alteration or addition to the Property or the installations in it carried out by the Tenant; or

(c) which it is the responsibility of the Tenant to do.

8.3 Notice of breaches

The Landlord is not liable to the Tenant for breach of this clause unless the Landlord fails to carry out the work within a reasonable period after the Tenant has given the Landlord notice of the breach.

9. ALTERATIONS

9.1 Except with the consent of the Landlord (and with whatever planning or building regulations consent may be necessary) the Tenant will not make alterations or additions or installations to or in the Property (or install any services in it) which may affect the structure or external appearance of the Property; and will make all alterations or additions for which consent may be given in conformity with the planning or building regulations consent required and to the satisfaction of the Landlord.

9.2 At the end of the lease (however it occurs) if so required by the Landlord the Tenant will remove any additions, alterations or installations made to or in the Property.

10. COMPLIANCE WITH STATUTES

10.1 Meaning of "statute"

In this condition, "statute" includes all existing and future Acts of Parliament, statutory instruments, regulations, orders or byelaws made under or in pursuance of any Act of Parliament.

10.2 General

The Tenant will observe and comply in all respects with the requirements of all statutes so far as they relate to or affect the Property.

10.3 Works required by statute

The Tenant will execute all works and provide and maintain all facilities, arrangements or other things which by or under any statute or by any government department, public or local authority or statutory undertaker or by the court are or may be directed or required to be executed, provided or maintained in or in respect of the Property.

10.4 Indemnity to Landlord

The Tenant will protect (that is, indemnify) the Landlord against all costs, charges and expenses of or incidental to the execution of any works or the provision or maintenance of any facilities, arrangements or other things directed or required and will not do any act at the Property by reason of which the Landlord may under any statute have imposed upon it or become liable to pay any penalty, damage, compensation, costs, charges or expense.

10.5 Planning requirements

The Tenant will comply in all respects with the provisions and requirements of the Town and Country Planning Acts for the time being in force whether in relation to the permitted use or otherwise and will protect (that is, indemnify) the Council against all liability whatsoever including costs and expenses in respect of any contravention.

10.6 Electrics inspection

The Tenant must arrange a periodic inspection of the electrical installations by an electrician approved by NICEIC and provide the Landlord with a copy of the inspection report carried out in the last six months of the term (however it may end) ensuring that the electrician has undertaken the works required to enable the installations to pass as satisfactory.

10.7 **Gas servicing**

In the last twelve months of the term (however it may end) the Tenant must arrange a service of the gas boiler and gas installations (if any) by an engineer on the Gas Safe Register, and provide the Landlord with a certificate of safety.

10.8 **Notices from authorities**

Upon receipt by the Tenant of a communication from a competent authority affecting or likely to affect the Property the Tenant will (so far as the communication or the Act, regulation or other instrument under or by virtue of which it is issued and the provisions of the lease require the tenant to do so) comply with it at the Tenant's expense and will immediately send the Landlord a copy of the communication.

10.9 **Scope of condition**

Obligations in this condition extend to all parts of the Property, to the use of the Property and to the employment in it of any chattel, substance or process.

11.   USE OF THE PROPERTY

11.1 **Permitted use**

The Tenant will not use the Property except for the use allowed.

11.2 **Change of use**

But with the consent of the Landlord (which may not be unreasonably withheld or delayed) the Tenant may change the use of the Property to another use which falls within class B1(c) of the schedule to the Town and Country Planning (Use Classes) Order 1987.

11.3 **Landlord may withhold consent**

It will be reasonable for the Landlord to withhold its consent where the Landlord reasonably considers—

(a)   that the proposed use would compete with and be to the detriment of any other use trade or business being carried on in any other of the Landlord's units at ► or (b)　　　that the proposed use is not suitable for or in keeping with the nature of the Landlord's units at ▶ or is not in accordance with the principles of good estate management or

(c)　　　that the proposed use would or might constitute or cause a breach of the following subcondition.

11.4　　**Express prohibitions**

In particular, the Tenant must not use the Property—

(a)　　　for a dangerous, radioactive, noxious or offensive trade, business or occupation

(b)　　　in a way which may be a nuisance, annoyance, disturbance or inconvenience to the Landlord its lessees, tenants or the owners or occupiers of neighbouring premises

(c)　　　as a betting office

(d)　　　for an illegal or immoral act or purpose

(e)　　　for a sale by auction

(f)　　　for a residential purpose, or

(g)　　　for retail trade of any kind.

11.5　　**Damage**

The Tenant must not cut, remove, alter or otherwise damage the Property; or the ceilings, walls, floors, girders, beams or timbers of the Property; or its wires, pipes, cables, drains and fixtures.

11.6　　**Overloading floors**

The Tenant must not overload the floors of the Property.

11.7　　**Abatement of nuisance**

The Landlord may give the Tenant a notice requiring the abatement of a nuisance caused by vibration, noise or smell, or by undue emission of smoke, gas, fumes, vapour or dust. The Tenant will then with all reasonable despatch comply with that notice.

11.8　　**Dangerous substances**

The Tenant will not store at or bring to the Property an article, substance or liquid of a radioactive, combustible, inflammable or dangerous nature.

11.9 **Asbestos**

The Tenant will not bring onto or use asbestos materials in or on the Property.

11.10 **Skips**

The Tenant will not bring or place a skip outside the Property without the Landlord's consent.

11.11 **External signs**

(a) Except with the consent of the Landlord, the Tenant will not display notices, posters or advertisements on the exterior of the Property (including the internal face of the external cladding of the building) or in the windows or doors of the Property.

(b) But the Tenant may display a trade sign on and of no greater dimension than the board affixed to the external wall for that purpose indicating the Tenant's name or trade name or logo and a description of the Tenant's business being carried on inside, and a telephone number. The form character and dimensions of the sign are to be approved by the Landlord in writing.

11.12 **Discharge into drains**

(a) The Tenant will not discharge into any pipe or drain serving the Property or any part of the ▶ [*insert name*] development any oil, grease, acid or other noxious, toxic or corrosive substance or any matter or thing which may cause an obstruction in or damage to that pipe or drain, or to which any water, sewerage or other competent authority may object.

(b) If any obstruction or damage occurs, the Tenant will immediately remedy it to the satisfaction of the Landlord.

(c) If a competent authority objects, the Tenant will immediately take the steps necessary to comply with the requirements of the competent authority.

11.13 **Storage outside**

The Tenant will ensure that no goods, equipment or materials are stored or otherwise placed outside or in the vicinity of the Property, except for refuse kept in proper receptacles.

11.14 Care of adjoining land

The Tenant must not make dirty the land, roads or pavements adjoining the Property, and in particular must not deposit refuse or other materials on them.

11.15 Masts and wires

The Tenant must not erect a pole, mast, or aerial or fix a cable or wire on the Property or install equipment on it, whether or not in connection with telecommunications.

12. DEALINGS WITH LEASE PROHIBITED

The Tenant must not assign, underlet, licence, part with possession or occupation or share possession or occupation of the Property or any part of it; nor hold it or any part of it in trust for another person.

13. PARKING AND SPEED LIMIT

13.1 Parking

(a)   The Tenant must ensure that between the hours of 8.30am and 5.30pm every day except Sundays and bank holidays no more than two cars or light vans are parked within the spaces coloured yellow on the attached plan, and then only by —

- the Tenant
- the Tenant's employees or agents; or
- any other person associated with the Tenant except visitors to the Property.

(b)   The Tenant must ensure that all visitors to the Property park their vehicles in the area coloured green on the attached plan.

(c)   Otherwise, the Tenant must not park a vehicle or trailer within ▶. But vehicles may park to load or unload, though the Tenant must ensure that no unnecessary obstruction is caused in ▶, in ▶ Road or in the vicinity.

13.2 Speed limit

(a)   Within seven days of the date of the lease, the Tenant must notify all his employees, agents and other persons associated with the Tenant, drawing attention to the speed limit of 15 mph imposed in ▶ and asking them to observe the speed limit at all times.

(b)   The Tenant must display in a prominent place in the Property at least one notice in a form approved by the Landlord in writing, reminding everyone leaving the Property of the speed limit and asking them to observe it.

(c)   The Tenant must ensure that new employees of the Tenant are given written notice of the speed limit within seven days of the start of their employment in accordance with the requirements of paragraph (a).

(d)   The Tenant must take all reasonable steps to ensure that all persons associated with the Tenant and all visitors and invitees to the Property observe the speed limit.

(e)   The Tenant must provide the Landlord on request with the evidence the Landlord may reasonably require of compliance by the Tenant with this subclause.

14.   PREVENT ENCROACHMENT

The Tenant will take all reasonable steps to prevent any encroachment upon the Property or the acquisition of a new easement over or under the Property, and will give notice to the Landlord of any threatened encroachment or attempt to acquire an easement as soon as the Tenant becomes aware of it.

15.   PROTECTION OF LANDLORD FROM CLAIMS

15.1   The Tenant will protect (that is, indemnify) the Landlord against the effect of damage, loss or injury caused to the Property or to adjacent or neighbouring premises or to any person.

15.2   In particular, the Tenant will protect (that is, indemnify) the Landlord from costs, claims and demands made against or incurred by the Landlord as a result of —

(a)   the Tenant's use and occupation of the Property or

(b)   any act, omission or negligence of the Tenant or the employees, agents licensees or invitees of the Tenant or

(c)   any breach or non-observance or non-performance by the Tenant of the obligations under the terms of the lease.

15.3   The preceding subconditions do not apply to the extent that the Landlord itself is negligent.

16. FIRE PRECAUTIONS

The Tenant will comply with all recommendations, requirements and directions of the Landlord, the fire authority and the Landlord's insurers relating to fire precautions relating to the Property and the means of escape from it in case of fire; and will ensure that the means of escape can be safely and effectively used at all times.

17. NOTICES AND VIEWINGS AT END OF TERM

During the last six months of the term (however it ends) the Tenant will —

(a) allow the Landlord to fix and retain notice boards of reasonable size to conspicuous parts of the Property announcing that it is to be let or disposed of, and

(b) at reasonable times of the day, allow all persons authorised by the Landlord to enter and view the Property.

18. YIELD UP

At the end of the term the Tenant must vacate the Property and hand it back to the Landlord together with all fixtures (tenant's fixtures excepted) in proper repair and condition, and decorated and repaired in accordance with the lease.

19. QUIET ENJOYMENT

The Landlord agrees with the Tenant that, provided the Tenant punctually pays the rent and observes the Tenant's obligations, the Tenant may peaceably use the Property without interruption by the Landlord or by anyone claiming under the Landlord.

20. INSURANCE

20.1 Insurance by Landlord

(a) The Landlord will insure the Property with a reputable insurer against—

- loss or damage by the insured risks in the sum which represents the full reinstatement cost, and

- professional fees and two years loss of rent.

(b) The Landlord's obligation under the preceding paragraph excludes all property of the Tenant, tenant's fixtures and plate glass which are the Tenant's responsibility to insure.

(c)   The Landlord need not maintain a separate policy of insurance for the Property but may insure by a block or general policy.

(d)   The Landlord will lay out all money received in respect of its insurance (except sums in respect of loss of rent or professional fees) in rebuilding or reinstating that part of the Property destroyed or damaged.

(e)   The Tenant may inspect the Landlord's insurance policy during normal office hours if the Tenant gives the Landlord at least seven days written notice.

20.2   **Tenant's obligations**

(a)   The Tenant will not do anything on the Property which might make void or voidable the insurance effected by the Landlord against the risk of damage or destruction by the insured risks of the Property or of any of the adjoining or neighbouring premises of the Landlord by which the premium for that insurance might be increased.

(b)   The Tenant will repay to the Landlord all sums paid by the Landlord in or about the renewal of any such policy rendered necessary by a breach of this covenant.

(c)   If the Property is damaged or destroyed by an insured risk during the term and the insurance money under the policy of insurance effected by the Landlord is irrecoverable through an act or default of the Tenant or the Tenant's employees or agents, the Tenant will pay to the Landlord the entire cost of rebuilding and reinstating the Property or (as the case may be) that proportion irrecoverable from the Landlord's insurers.

21.   **SUSPENSION OF RENT IF PROPERTY DAMAGED OR DESTROYED BY INSURED RISKS**

21.1   If the Property is destroyed or so damaged by any of the insured risks as to be unfit for occupation and use, then subject to the following subclause, the rent (or a fair proportion of the rent according to the nature and extent of the damaged sustained) will be suspended until whichever of the following events occurs first:

    (a)   the Property, in the reasonable opinion of the Landlord, is again fit for occupation and use

    (b)   expiry of the period covered by any loss-of-rent insurance

(c)   expiry of a notice of election given by either the Landlord or the Tenant under the next main clause (ending the lease if the Property is destroyed or damaged).

21.2   But this does not apply if —

(a)   the Property is destroyed or damaged by the act, default or negligence of the Tenant, or of the Tenant's employees, agents or visitors; or

(b)   the insurance effected by the Landlord has been invalidated, or payment of the policy money refused in whole or in part, in consequence of some act or default of the Tenant or the Tenant's employees, agents or visitors.

22.   ENDING LEASE IF THE PROPERTY IS DESTROYED OR DAMAGED

22.1   If the Property is destroyed or so damaged by any of the insured risks as to be unfit for occupation and use and it cannot be reinstated without substantial rebuilding, the Landlord may elect to treat the lease as at an end and re-enter the Property on giving to the Tenant at least six months notice of that election.

22.2   If the Landlord has not begun to reinstate the Property within the six months following the destruction or damage, the Tenant may elect to treat the lease as at an end and vacate the Property on giving to the Landlord not less than one month's notice of that election.

22.3   Any termination under this clause does not affect the rights of any party to recover in respect of any breach of any of the terms of the lease.

22.4   On service of a notice of election to treat the lease as at an end by either the Landlord or the Tenant, all money received from the insurance effected by the Landlord under the lease belongs to the Landlord absolutely.

23.   SERVICES

The Landlord will provide the services specified in schedule 3.

24.   FORFEITURE OF THE LEASE

24.1   Each of the following is a forfeiting event within the meaning of this clause:

(a) the rent or any other sum payable by the Tenant under the lease is in arrears and unpaid for twenty one days after becoming payable (whether formally demanded or not)

(b) there is a breach by the Tenant of any of the tenant covenants in the lease

(c) a proposal is made in respect of the Tenant for a voluntary arrangement for a composition of debts or for a scheme of arrangement approved in accordance with the Insolvency Act 1986

(d) the Tenant becomes bankrupt

(e) an application is made to the court under the Insolvency Act 1986 in respect of the Tenant (being a company) for the appointment of an administrator

(f) the Tenant (being a company) enters into liquidation whether compulsory or voluntary (but not if the liquidation is for reconstruction of a solvent company) or has a receiver or manager of its business or undertaking, or has an administrative receiver (as defined in the Insolvency Act 1986) appointed, or

(g) the Tenant suffers any distress or execution to be levied on the Tenant's goods.

24.2 If and whenever a forfeiting event occurs, the Landlord may re-enter the Property at any time and the lease then comes to an end. Re-entry on part is to be treated as re-entry on the whole.

24.3 This right arises even if a previous right of re-entry has been waived.

24.4 Where the Tenant consists of more than one person, this right arises when a forfeiting event happens to one or more of them.

24.5 The ending of the lease under this clause does not affect the rights of any party in relation to any breach of the terms of the lease which occurred before the lease ended.

25. TENANT'S RIGHT TO BREAK

25.1 Provided the preconditions below are met, the Tenant may terminate the lease —

(a)   after the expiry of the first six months of the term, and

(b)   before the start of the last six months of the term.

25.2   The Tenant must give the Landlord three months notice of termination.

25.3   Subject to the preceding sub clause, the notice may expire at any time and not necessarily on a day for payment of rent.

25.4   The first precondition is that on and before the notice is given, the Tenant must have paid all rent and other sums due to the Landlord under the lease.

25.5   The second precondition is that on or before the expiry date of the notice, the Tenant must —

(a)   have paid to the Landlord all rent and other sums due up to and including the expiry date of the notice, and

(b)   give vacant possession of the Property.

25.6   The Tenant has no right to compensation for the unexpired part of the term if it terminates under this clause, but a party may recover for breach of a provision of the lease.

25.7   As soon as practicable after termination the Landlord will repay to the Tenant any rent or other money paid in advance for a period after termination.

26.   TENANT'S COMPENSATION ON QUITTING

Subject to the provisions of section 38(2) of the Landlord and Tenant Act 1954, the Tenant is not entitled on vacating the Property to any compensation under section 37 of that Act.

27.   NOTICES

27.1   In these conditions a notice includes a consent, request, demand and notification.

27.2   A notice under the lease must be given in writing.

27.3   The notice will be taken to be received —

(a)   on delivery, if served by hand

(b)   two working days after posting if sent by ordinary first-class post, unless it is returned undelivered

(c)   on the day of sending, if sent by recorded delivery post

(d)   on the day sent by fax, if sent before 3pm

(e)   on the next working day after being sent by fax if sent at 3pm or later.

27.4   Sending by email does not constitute good service under the lease.

27.5   The notice is taken to be delivered as follows:

(a)   to the Landlord, if left for or sent to ▶

(b)   to an individual Tenant, if left for or sent to the Tenant at the address given in this lease or at the Property or at the Tenant's last known address or place of business in the United Kingdom

(c)   to a company Tenant, if left for or sent to the Tenant at the Tenant's registered office or the Property

(d)   to an individual guarantor, if left for or sent to the guarantor at the address given in the lease or at the guarantor's last known address or place of business in the United Kingdom

(e)   to a company guarantor, if left for or sent to the guarantor at the guarantor's registered office or at the guarantor's last known address or place of business in the United Kingdom.

28.   LANDLORD'S RIGHT TO USE ADJOINING OR NEIGHBOURING LAND AND BUILDINGS

28.1   The Landlord is entitled to deal as it thinks fit with any adjoining or neighbouring premises of the Landlord and to erect, or have erected, on those adjoining or neighbouring premises any buildings whatsoever, whether those buildings do or do not affect or diminish the light or air which may be enjoyed by the Property.

28.2   Nothing in the lease imposes any restriction on the use of any land or building not included in this lease. Nor does the Tenant have any standing in relation to the grant, enforcement, release or modification of land, assets or rights of any tenant or licensee of the Landlord relating to land or buildings not including in the lease.

29. LANDLORD'S NON-LIABILITY FOR ACCIDENTS ON THE PROPERTY

29.1 The Landlord is not responsible to the Tenant or to anyone on the Property for —

(a) accident or injury on the Property, including injury resulting in death; and

(b) damage or loss to an asset on the Property.

29.2 This does not apply to the extent that the accident, injury, damage or loss occurs as a result of negligence on the part of the Landlord.

30. NO ENFORCEMENT BY NON-PARTY

A person who is not a party to the lease has no right to enforce any of its terms.

31. GUARANTOR'S OBLIGATIONS

31.1 Main duty

If the Tenant defaults on a tenant covenant in the lease (including default on payment of rent or other money) the Guarantor must perform that covenant.

31.2 No release of Guarantor

None of the following release or in any way affect the liability of the Guarantor under this Condition:

(a) grant by the Landlord of time or other indulgence to the Tenant

(b) neglect or abstention by the Landlord in enforcement of a tenant covenant

(c) refusal by the Landlord to accept rent at a time when it is reasonably considered that to do so might amount to waiver of a right to forfeit

(d) variation of the lease

(e) surrender of part of the Property (in which case the liability of the Guarantor extends only to the part of the Property not surrendered)

(f) any other happening by which, apart from this clause, the Guarantor would have been released.

31.3 Disclaimer of lease

This guarantee continues after any disclaimer of the lease by a trustee in bankruptcy or liquidator until the Property has been relet by the Landlord.

31.4 Guarantor a principal debtor

The Guarantor is liable to the Landlord as a principal debtor.

SCHEDULE 1

RIGHTS GRANTED

The following rights are granted to the Tenant (in common with the Landlord and all other persons having the like right) at all times and for all purposes connected with the Property.

(1) **Access**

The right of access to and from the Property with or without vehicles over the land coloured blue on the attached plan

(2) **Rubbish**

The right to place rubbish in the receptacles provided by the Landlord on the land coloured red on the attached plan

(3) **Services**

The right of free and uninterrupted passage and running of gas, electricity, telephone, water, sewage and other services to and from the Property into, through and along the drains, pipes, wires and cables now laid or laid during the term over the adjoining land of the Landlord, subject to the Tenant complying with condition 11.12 (discharge into drains).

(4) **Parking**

The right to park cars and vehicles in those of the car parking spaces on the land coloured yellow on the attached plan as may be available from time to time.

SCHEDULE 2

RIGHTS RESERVED

THERE are excepted and reserved out of this letting to the Landlord and all others lawfully authorised all rights and privileges now enjoyed over or against the Property and the following particular rights.

(1)   **Services now**

Rights in respect of the Property for the benefit of the remainder of and all persons from time to time in that building corresponding to those granted to the Tenant in paragraph (3) of schedule 1.

(2)   **Future services**

The right to construct and maintain in over or under the Property any easements or services for the benefit of adjacent premises.

(3)   **Entry**

The right at any time during the term on reasonable prior notice to the Tenant (except in an emergency) to enter (or in an emergency during the Tenant's absence to break and enter) the Property —

(a)   to inspect or execute works in connection with any of the easements or services excepted and reserved by paragraph (1) above or

(b)   to view the condition of the Property or

(c)   to execute works upon any adjacent premises in connection with which there is reserved also the right to build on or into any external wall of the Property or

(d)   to execute any repairs or other works which should or may be executed by the Landlord or any other person so authorised under the provisions of the lease or

(e)   to carry out the Landlord's obligations under the lease.

(4)   **Works on premises nearby**

The right at any time during the term to undertake other works upon any adjacent premises in such manner as the person exercising such right may think fit, despite interference with the access of light and air to the Property and without any liability to pay compensation.

(5)   **Building on external walls**

The right to build on or into an external wall of the Property.

(6)   **Scaffolding**

The right to erect and maintain scaffolding to repair or clean the exterior of [▶ *insert name*]. This right is exercisable even if the scaffolding might temporarily interfere with access to or the use of the Property, though the interference must be for the minimum reasonable period and access to the Property must not be completely obstructed.

The person exercising any of these rights —

(a)   is to cause as little damage as practicable, and

(b)   is to make good all damage caused to the Property straight away, but

(c)   is not liable to pay compensation.

SCHEDULE 3

SERVICES

(1)   **Painting**

The painting of all parts of the exterior of the Property at the times the Landlord considers desirable.

(2)   **Open areas**

The cleaning, maintenance, lighting (if appropriate) and repair of the forecourt and car parking area and the landscaped areas.

(3)   **Refuse**

The provision of refuse bins.

SCHEDULE 4

RENT DEPOSIT

(1)   **Rent deposit paid**

The Tenant has handed the rent deposit to the Landlord (and the Landlord acknowledges receipt of it) to be held by the Landlord on the terms of this schedule.

(2)   **Application of rent deposit**

(a)   The Landlord is entitled at any time to apply the whole or part of the rent deposit in payment of an amount owing to the Landlord as a result of the failure by the Tenant to pay—

- the whole or part of the rents reserved by the lease

- other money (including interest on rent arrears) payable under the lease

- a cost or expense incurred by or payable to the Landlord in consequence of failure by the Tenant to observe the obligations on the Tenant under the lease.

(a)   Before applying any part of the rent deposit, the Landlord will first give the Tenant at least seven days written notice of its intention to do so. In that notice, the Landlord will specify the amount to be applied and the date on which the application is to be made.

(3)   **Charge of rent deposit**

The Tenant charges the rent deposit in favour of the Landlord as security for performance of the Tenant's obligations in the lease and in this schedule.

(4)   **Topping up rent deposit**

(a)   The Tenant covenants with the Landlord during the term of the lease to maintain the rent deposit at the figure given on page 1.

(b)   Whenever the Landlord applies any part of the rent deposit under paragraph (2), the Tenant will within seven days of the date specified in the Landlord's notice pay over to the Landlord a sum equal to the amount specified in the notice.

(c)   A sum not paid within that seven-day period bears interest at 5% over the base lending rate from time to time of the Landlord's bank. Interest runs in the period beginning with the date specified in the Landlord's notice and ending with the date of payment.

(5)   **Return of rent deposit**

The Landlord will return the balance of the rent deposit (after first being applied in satisfaction of claims by the Landlord in accordance with paragraph (2)) to the Tenant without interest when the lease comes to an end (however that is brought about).

(6)   **Special points**

To avoid misunderstandings—

(a)   the Tenant is not entitled to interest on the rent deposit

(b)   the liability of the Tenant is not limited to the rent deposit

(c)   the rights of the Landlord under this schedule do not restrict the other rights of the Landlord under the lease, and

(d)   the proviso for re-entry in the lease is exercisable on breach by the Tenant of an obligation in this schedule as well as on the happening of the other events mentioned in the lease.

< Conditions end>

REFERENCES AND FURTHER READING

Listed here are some of the works referred to in this guide together with a small selection of other useful material.

Published material

Adler M & Perry D., *Clarity for Lawyers* (Law Society Publishing, London, 3rd ed., 2017)

Aitken J.K. & Butt, P., *Piesse: Elements of Drafting* (Lawbook Co., Australia, 10th ed., 2004)

Asprey M., *Plain Language for Lawyers* (Federation Press, Sydney, 4th ed., 2010)

Butt P., *Modern Legal Drafting - A Guide to Using Clearer Language* (Cambridge University Press, 3rd ed., 2013)

Dickerson R., *Fundamentals of Legal Drafting* (Little, Brown & Co, Boston and Toronto, 2nd ed., 1986)

Greenberg D., *Craies on Legislation* (Sweet and Maxwell, London, 11th ed., 2018)

Kessler J. and John C., *Drafting Trusts and Will Trusts* (Sweet and Maxwell, London, 14th ed., 2019)

Xanthaki H., *Thornton's Legislative Drafting* (Butterworths, London, 5th ed., 2013)

Material from drafting offices

Australia

Office of Parliamentary Counsel, Australian Government, *Plain English Manual,* available at www.opc.gov.au/plain/docs.htm

 Law Reform Commission of Victoria, *Plain English and the Law*, 1987, Appendix 1 – "Guidelines for Drafting in Plain English: A Manual for Legislative Drafters"

Canada

Department of Justice, *Legistics*, available at www.justice.gc.ca/ eng/dept-min/pub/ legis/index.html

United Kingdom

Office of the Parliamentary Counsel : Drafting Guidance (https:// www.gov.uk/government/publications/drafting-bills-for-parliament)

Tax Law Rewrite: The Way Forward: Annex 1 - Guidelines for the Rewrite was a useful guide, but now appears to be unobtainable.

Plain Language and Legislation (Scottish Government) (https:// www2.gov.scot/resource/doc/93488/0022476.pdf)

ABOUT THE AUTHOR

Richard William Castle qualified as a lawyer in the 1960s. He has specialised in property transactions, especially leases. In the 1980s he joined the plain English movement and was a founder-member of Clarity, an international association promoting plain legal language. He has published a number of books and articles, and studied and lived for many years in Cambridge. He now lives and works in Tetbury, Gloucestershire, and remains a visiting fellow in the Department of Land Economy, University of Cambridge. His website can be found at:

<https://sites.google.com/site/richardcastlelawyer/>

INDEX

BV - #0116 - 220426 - C265 - 229/152/14 - PB - 9781861519535 - Gloss Lamination